SOLVE THE PROBLEMS IN SHORT-CUT METHODS

by
B.N.R. Krishnan

SURA COLLEGE OF COMPETITION

Chennai • Tirunelveli • Ernakulam
• Thiruvananthapuram • Bengalooru

© PUBLISHERS

SOLVE THE PROBLEMS IN SHORT-CUT METHODS

by
B.N.R. Krishnan

This Edition : March, 2016
Size : 1/8 Demy
Pages : 96

ISBN : 81-7254-034-5
Code : C 11

[NO ONE IS PERMITTED TO COPY OR TRANSLATE IN ANY OTHER LANGUAGE THE CONTENTS OF THIS BOOK OR PART THEREOF IN ANY FORM WITHOUT THE WRITTEN PERMISSION OF THE PUBLISHERS]

SURA COLLEGE OF COMPETITION

Head Office: 1620, 'J' Block, 16th Main Road, Anna Nagar, **Chennai - 600 040.** Phones: 044-26162173, 26161099.

Branches :
- KAP Complex, I Floor, 20, Trivandrum Road, **Tirunelveli - 627 002.** Phone : 0462-4200557
- 35/1465, Kochaneth Tower, Ground Floor, Ratnam Lane, South Janatha Road, Palarivattom, **Ernakulam - 682 025.** Phones: 0484-3205797, 2535636
- TC 28/2816, Sriniketan, Kuthiravattam Road, **Thiruvananthapuram - 695 001.** Phone: 0471-4063864
- 3638/A, 4th Cross, Opp. to Malleswaram Railway Station, Gayathri Nagar, Back gate of Subramaniya Nagar, **Bengalooru - 560 021.** Phone: 080-23324950

Printed at G.T. Krishna Press, Chennai - 600 102 and Published by
V.V.K.Subburaj for Sura College of Competition
1620, 'J' Block, 16th Main Road, Anna Nagar, Chennai - 600 040.
Phones: 26162173, 26161099. Fax: (91) 44-26162173.
e-mail: enquiry@surabooks.com; website: www.surabooks.com

CONTENTS

		Pages
1.	RATIO AND PROPORTION	1
2.	NUMERATOR AND DENOMINATOR	8
3.	AGES	16
4.	PROFIT AND LOSS	20
5.	MISCELLANEOUS	26
6.	AVERAGES	33
7.	PERCENTAGES	41
8.	TIME AND DISTANCE	62
9.	TIME AND WORK	78
10.	INTEREST	85

RATIO AND PROPORTION

MIXTURES

1. In what proportion should water and milk be mixed to reduce the price of milk from Rs.5 to Rs.3 per litre.

   Ans : $(5-3):3 = 2:3$ water : milk

2. A man buys 16 litres of milk at Rs.4.80 per litre and adds 4 litres of water. If he wants a profit of $12\frac{1}{2}$% at what rate should he sell the mixture?

   Ans: $12\frac{1}{2}$% is $\frac{1}{8}$.

   $\therefore$ S.P of milk = Rs.4.80 + Rs.0.60 = Rs.5.40.

   New S.P Rate = $\frac{16 \text{ (OLD QTY)}}{20 \text{ (NEW QTY)}} \times$ Rs.5.40 = $\frac{4}{5} \times 5.40$

   = Rs.4.32 per litre.

3. A 10 Litre Tin is full of milk which consists 5% of water. 4 litres of this milk is removed and in its place the same quantity of water is added. What is the percentage of milk in the new mixture?

   Ans: In the balance of 6 litres of milk, the milk was 95% (since 5% was water) i.e. $6 \times \frac{95}{100} = 3 \times \frac{19}{10} = \frac{57}{10} = 5.7$ litres. After adding water, there is no change in the QTY of milk.

   New % of milk = $\frac{5.7}{M6 + 4W} \times 100 = 57\%$

4. There are 2 vessels full of milk with milk and water ratio 1:3 and 3:5 respectively. If both are mixed in the ratio 3:2, what would be the ratio of milk and water in the new mixture?

   Ans: Have equal quantities of both varieties and their ratios will be 2:6(8) and 3:5(8). Take 3 units of the 1st and 2 units of the second, and quantities will be 6:18 and 6:10. Therefore, the M & W in the new mixture will be in ratio $(6+6):(18+10) = 12:28 = 3:7$.

5. In 2 varieties of Alcohol, the Alcohol and water are in the ratio 3:5 and 7:3 respectively. In what proportion the two must be mixed to get a new mixture with A:W ratio 5:3?

Ans : It is enough to take either Alcohol or Water side. Take alcohol side. Ist $\frac{3}{8}$, new mix $\frac{5}{8}$ & 2nd mix $\frac{7}{10}$ all Alcohol.

(or) $\frac{15}{40}$ $\frac{25}{40}$ $\frac{28}{40}$

(or) 15   25   28

∴ Ratio in which to be mixed = (28 – 25) : (25 – 15) = 3 : 10

6. In a mixture the milk and water ratio was 3:2. After 8 litres of milk and 10 litres of water is added, the new ratio of M:W is 4:3. What was the original quantity?

Ans : New Ratio $\overset{MW}{4:3}$ (A:B) $\dfrac{\text{Diff between A} \times \text{D and B} \times \text{C}}{\text{Diff between B} \times \text{E and A} \times \text{F}}$

Qty added 8:10 (C:D)

Orig. Ratio 3:2 (E:F)

$= \dfrac{40-24}{9-8}$ = 16 times of original Ratio 3:2

= 48M 32W in original mixture.

Total original quantity = 80 litres

7. In 120 litres of Alcohol, the strength of Alcohol was 60%. Some quantity was stolen and same quantity of water was substituted. If the strength of Alcohol is now 50%, what quantity was stolen?

Ans : Stolen quantity $= \dfrac{60-50}{60} = \dfrac{10}{60} = \dfrac{1}{6}$ th part = 20 litres.

If % is asked $\dfrac{1}{6} \times 100 = 16\dfrac{2}{3}\%$ was stolen.

8. The strength of milk in a quantity of 120 litres is 70%. If 12 litres of water is added to this, what will be the percentage of milk in the new mixture?

Ans : Note, there is no change in the quantity of milk.

$\dfrac{\text{Old Qty}}{\text{New Qty}} \times \text{strength of milk} = \dfrac{120}{132} \times 70 = \dfrac{700}{11} = 63\dfrac{7}{11}\%$.

Note that 12 litres is $\dfrac{1}{11}$ of the new quantity and so the percentage of strength of milk falls by $\dfrac{70}{11} = 6\dfrac{4}{11}\%$.

9. In 150 litres of Alcohol, the Alcohol and Water are mixed in ratio 3:2. If 30 litres of water is added, what is the ratio of Alcohol and water in the new mixture?

Ans : There is no change in Alcohol quantity.

so $\dfrac{150}{180} \times \dfrac{3}{5} = \dfrac{5}{6} \times \dfrac{3}{5} = \dfrac{1}{2}$ is Alcohol.

Other part of $\dfrac{1}{2}$ is water. So ratio is 1:1.

10. An adulterated quantity of milk has 75% milk. When 4 lit. of water is added, the strength of milk falls to 70%. What is the original quantity?

Ans : $\dfrac{\text{New\%} \times \text{Qty of water added}}{\text{Diff in\%}} = \dfrac{70 \times 4}{5} = 56$ lit.

11. 2 varieties of Sugar costing Rs.5 and Rs.6 per kilo were bought in ratio 2:3 and entire quantity was sold at Rs.6.50 per kilo. If the profit was Rs.13.50, how much quantity of each was bought?

Ans : Quantity = 2:3 Profit ratio = Rs.1.50 : 0.50*

Multiply $2 \times 1.50 : 3 \times 0.50 = 3$ and $1\dfrac{1}{2}$

Unit Times = $\dfrac{\text{Rs.}13.50}{3 + 1\dfrac{1}{2}}$ = 3 times of given Ratio.

∴ Qty. of sugar bought at Rs.5 ---- $3 \times 2 = 6$ kilos.

Qty. of sugar bought at Rs.6 ---- $3 \times 3 = 9$ kilos.

*We do not change the ratio because the profit is definite.

12. The strength of milk in 3 vessels containing adulterated milk are 50%, 60%, and 80% respectively. If 4 litres, 6 litres and 2 litres respectively are taken from the 3 vessels and mixed, what would be the milk and water ratio in the new mixture?

Ans: It is enough to take milk side:

Milk in 12 litres (4 + 6 + 2)

$= 50\%$ of 4 + 60% of 6 + 80% of 2

$= 2 + 3.6 + 1.6 = 7.2$

% of milk $= \dfrac{7.2}{12} \times 100 = 60\%$

∴ 40% water Their ratio 3 : 2

Note : In the problem, instead of percentages the ratios may be given as 1:1; 3:2; 4:1; (or) the milk as $\frac{1}{2}$ part, $\frac{3}{5}$ part, $\frac{4}{5}$ part. Working method is the same.

13. A trader buys some litres of alcohol at Rs.6 per litre and after adding 7 litres of water sells the mixture at Rs.5 per litre. If he gains $12\frac{1}{2}$ % in the process, what was the original quantity bought by him?

    Ans : With C.P Rs.6 and profit $\frac{1}{8}$ the S.P. is Rs.6.75.
    Difference in
    S.P per litre = 6.75 − 5 = Rs.1.75.

    $$\text{Original quantity} = \frac{7 \times 5}{1.75} = \frac{35}{1.75} = 20 \text{ litres.}$$

14. In what ratio two varieties of sugar costing Rs.3.50 per kilo and Rs.4.50 per kilo must be mixed to have a rate of Rs.4.20 per kilo.

    Ans : The increase of 70 paise on the first is to be compensated by the decrease of 30 paise on the second.

    Ratio = 30 : 70 (i.e.) 3 : 7

15. 2 varieties of sugar at Rs.6 per kilo and Rs.4 per kilo respectively were bought for a total sum of Rs.240. If these two varieties were bought at Rs.5 and Rs.5 respectively, it would have cost Rs.10 more. How much of each variety was bought?

    Ans :

GR I	GR II
6	4(240) or A3 B2 (120) E
5	5(250) or C1 D1 (50)F

    $$\text{GR I} = \frac{\text{Diff between B} \times \text{F and D} \times \text{E} (\sim)}{\text{Diff between A} \times \text{D and B} \times \text{C} (\sim)}$$

    $$= \frac{120 - 100}{1} = 20 \text{ Kg.}$$

    $$\text{II} = \frac{(3 \times 50) - (1 \times 120)}{3 - 2} = \frac{30}{1} = 30 \text{ Kg.}$$

    [follow the same method if quantity is given and rates are to be found.]

16. A man buys 60Kg, of sugar and sells $\frac{1}{2}$ of it at 10% profit, $\frac{1}{3}$ of it at 5% profit and balance at 20% profit. His total profit was Rs.30. What is the C.P.?

Ans : (A) Qty :- $\frac{1}{2}$ $\frac{1}{3}$ Bal $\frac{1}{6}$

(B) Profit :-   10   5   20

A × B Ratio - $5 : \frac{5}{3} : \frac{20}{6}$ (or) 30 : 10 : 20 (or) 3 : 1 : 2

Total CP of 6 units = Rs.30. ∴ CP of 1Kg = Rs.5

Consider that: Qty of 60Kg in ratio $\frac{1}{2} : \frac{1}{3} : \frac{1}{6}$ (or) 3:2:1 will be 30Kg, 20Kg, 10Kg. Profit of 10%, 5% and 20% respectively mean a gain of 3Kg, 1Kg, and 2Kg respectively. So gain of 6Kg is equal to Rs.30. Cost of 1Kg = Rs.5.

17. A trader bought 100 Bananas, some at 5 for Re.1, and rest at 6 per rupee and sold all of them at 4 for 1 Re. If his overall gain was Rs.7, how many Bananas he bought at different rates?

Ans : Amount got by sale = $\frac{100}{4}$ = Rs.25.

Cost price = 25 – 7 = Rs.18.

1. If all were bought at 5 per rupee - cost = $\frac{100}{5}$ = Rs.20

2. If all were bought at 6 per Rupee - cost = $\frac{100}{6}$ = Rs.$16\frac{2}{3}$

Cost 1. 20 overall 2. $16\frac{2}{3}$
           18

So ratio of quantity at 5 & 6 respectively

$\left(18 - 16\frac{2}{3}\right) : (20 - 18) = \left(1\frac{1}{3} : 2\right) = 4 : 6 = 2 : 3$.

∴ 40 at 5 for Re.1 & 60 at 6 per Re.1

18. The ratio of students who passed and failed in 6th std exam was 2:3 and that in std 7th was 3:2. If the failed students in 6th and 7th std, are in the ratio 6:5 and if there are 60 students in 6th std, how many students are there in 7th std?

Ans : Failed in 6th std $= 60 \times \dfrac{3}{5} = 36$

Ratio 6 : 5 can be written as 36 : 30

∴ Failed in 7th std $= 30$ students $= \dfrac{2}{5}$ th of class

Students in 7th std $= 30 \times \dfrac{5}{2} = 75$.

19. In a mixture, milk strength is 60%. After 10 litres of milk is added, the water strength becomes 20%. What was the original quantity?

    Ans :

	M	W
Original	60	40 or 3 : 2
New	80	20 or 4 : 1 or 8 : 2

    Water is made common as no quantity of it was added.

    If $(8 - 3) = 5$ litres of milk is added, the original quantity is $(3 + 2) = 5$ litres.

    If 10 litres of milk is added, the original quantity = 10 litres.

20. In 50Kg, of Ghee, 30% is Vanaspati. How much Ghee is to be added to make the Ghee strength 80%.

    Ans : 50Kgs - G - V   G - V

    70% - 30%   35 15 = 7 : 3

    After adding, Ghee 80% - Vanaspathi 20%

    G : V = 4 : 1

    Old ratio - 7 : 3

    New ratio - 4 : 1 or 12 : 3. As no Vanaspati is added make it common.

    If original $(7+3) = 10$ Units, added qty. is $(12-7) = 5$Kgs. As original was 50Kgs, added quantity of Ghee was $5 \times 5 = 25$.

    There is no change in Vanaspati. So the new mixture of 75Kgs has $(35 + 25) = 60$Kg of Ghee and 15Kg of Vanaspati.

21. **A jarful of adulterated milk contains 50% water. 15% of it was removed and water was poured to fill the jar. Again 20% of quantity was removed and water was filled in its place. What is the percentage of milk in jarful of milk.**

Ans : When 15% was removed, 85% remained. Again when 20% was removed, 80% of balance remained. But, the jar contained even in the beginning only 50% of milk.

So the new strength of milk

$$= \frac{1}{2}\left[\frac{85}{100} \times \frac{80}{100} \times 100\right] = \frac{1}{2}(68) = 34\%$$

Note : There is no need to assume the quantity of milk as x litres. The actual quantity makes no difference.

NUMERATOR DENOMINATOR

1. In a fraction the Denominator is 20 more than the Numerator. If 10 is added to both, the new fraction will be $\frac{3}{7}$. What is the fraction?

   Ans : $A = 20$; $B = 10$; $\frac{3}{7} = \frac{C}{D}$

   Numerator $= \frac{A \times C - B(D - C)}{D - C} = \frac{60 - 40}{4} = 5$ so

   Denominator $= 25$, Fraction $\frac{5}{25}$

   Note : Denominator is directly got by

   $\frac{A \times D - B(D - C)}{D - C} = \frac{140 - 40}{4} = 25$. So Num $= 5$.

   The above too is a mental process. Another mental process is - Difference of $7 - 3 = 4$ Units which is equal to 20. So 1 unit $= 5$.

   Therefore, the future fraction will be $\frac{5 \times 3}{5 \times 7} = \frac{15}{35}$

   So, present figure is $\frac{5}{25}$

   Note : It may be stated in the problem that the Numerator is 20 LESS than the Denominator. Same method of working is to be followed.

2. The Numerator and Denominator of a fraction are in ratio 3 : 5. If 12 is added to both, their ratio will be 3 : 4. What is the fraction?

   Ans : (A) 3 (B) 5 For original fraction

   (C) 3 (D) 4

   (E) 12 $\frac{E \times (D - C)}{A \times D \sim B \times C} \times 3 : 5$

   ($\sim$) means deduct lower Number from higher Number.

   $= \frac{12 \times 1}{3} = 4$ ∴ The original fraction is $\frac{4 \times 3}{4 \times 5} = \frac{12}{20}$

Note that the new fraction is got by $\dfrac{12 \times (5-3)}{3} = 8$ times of 3 : 4. The new fraction will be $\dfrac{8 \times 3}{8 \times 4} = \dfrac{24}{32}$

3. The ratio of Numerator:Denominator is 5 : 8. If 8 is deducted from both, the new ratio will be 1: 2. What is the original fraction?

   Ans : $\dfrac{5}{1} \quad \dfrac{8}{2} \quad \dfrac{8 \times (2-1)}{5 \times 2 \sim 8 \times 1} = \dfrac{8}{2} = 4$ times 5:8

   $\qquad\qquad\qquad\qquad\qquad = \dfrac{20}{32}$ Pl. see also problem (2).

4. In a fraction the Numerator is 4 less than Denominator. If 6 is deducted from both, the fraction will be $\dfrac{5}{7}$. What is the original fraction?

   Ans: $A = 4;\ B = 6;\ \dfrac{C}{D} = \dfrac{5}{7}\quad \dfrac{A \times C + B \times (D - C)}{D - C}$

   Original Numerator = $\dfrac{4 \times 5 + 6\,(2)}{2} = \dfrac{32}{2} = 16$

   so, original fraction = $\dfrac{16}{20}$ Pl. see problem (1)

5. $\dfrac{2}{3}$ of a Number is 6 more than $\dfrac{5}{9}$ of the Number. Find the Number.

   Ans : $\dfrac{A}{B} = \dfrac{2}{3}\ \ C = 6\ \ \dfrac{D}{E} = \dfrac{5}{9}$ Then $\dfrac{B \times C \times E}{B \times D \sim A \times E}$

   $= \dfrac{3 \times 6 \times 9}{15 \sim 18} = \dfrac{162}{3} = 54$

   (or) simply $\dfrac{2}{3} - \dfrac{5}{9} = \dfrac{1}{9}$ th = 6

   Number = 54

   Note : Same method is to be followed if 'less than' is given instead of 'more than' in the sum.

5. A number when divided by $\dfrac{4}{5}$ gives a result $\dfrac{27}{32}$ more than the result obtained by multiplying the same number by $\dfrac{4}{5}$. What is the number?

Divide by $\frac{4}{5}$ means multiply by $\frac{5}{4}$.

Multiply $\frac{5(C)}{4(A)}$ Multiply $\frac{4(D)}{5(B)}$ More $\frac{27}{32}$

Number required $= \frac{A \times B \times 27}{C + D \times 32} = \frac{20 \times 27}{9 \times 32} = \frac{540}{288} = \frac{60}{32}$

$= \frac{15}{8}$. Its a fraction.

6. If the Numerator and Denominator of a fraction are each increased by 5, the fraction will become $\frac{5}{6}$. If they are each reduced by 16, the fraction becomes $\frac{3}{5}$. Find the fraction. (In such problems both x,y are used)

Ans : Note that the difference between 2 extremes is

$5 + 16 = 21$ each in 'Numerator' and 'Denominator'.

So, we may say fraction represented by $\frac{3 \text{ ADD } 21}{5 \text{ ADD } 21}$ we get fraction represented by $\frac{5}{6}$

Write like this :- (A) 3 (B) 5

(C) 21 (D) 21

(E) 5 (F) 6

$\frac{\text{Diff between } A \times D \text{ and } B \times C}{\text{Diff between } A \times F \text{ and } B \times E} = \frac{105 - 63}{25 - 18} = \frac{42}{7} = 6$ times.

6 times of both $\frac{5}{6} = \frac{30}{36}$

So $\frac{30}{36} \frac{-21}{-21} = \frac{9}{15}$

Required fraction $= \frac{30 - 5}{36 - 5} = \frac{25}{31}$

Note that if we take the difference between $C \times F$ & $D \times C$ we have to multiply 3 : 5 or $\frac{3}{5}$ by the Number of times got

$\frac{21 \times 6 - 21 \times 5}{5 \times 5 - 3 \times 6} = \frac{126 - 105}{7} = 3$ times of $\frac{3}{5} = \frac{9}{15}$

as required fraction $= \frac{9 + 16}{15 + 16} = \frac{25}{31}$

7. The Numerator is 6 less than Denominator. If 15 is deducted both from Numerator and Denominator, the fraction becomes $\frac{1}{3}$. What is the original fraction?

   Ans : Pl. see problem (4)

   $3 - 1 = 2$ units, $\frac{6}{2} = 3$ times.

   Fraction after deduction $= \frac{3 \times 1}{3 \times 3} = \frac{3}{9}$.

   Original fraction : $\frac{3+15}{9+15} = \frac{18}{24}$

   Note : the mental process of working.

8. A has 6 Rupees less than what B has. After each of them spent Rs.15, the balances are in ratio 1:3 respectively. How much money they had in the beginning?

   Ans : Same method as above.

9. Seetha had Rs.20 more than Geetha. After each of them was given Rs.10 by their father, the money with them was in ratio 3:7. How much money each had in the beginning?

   Ans : Same method as in problem (1)

10. A father gave pocket money to his two daughters in such a way that $\frac{2}{3}$ of it to Latha and $\frac{5}{9}$ of it to Geeta. If Latha got Rs.6 more, what was the amount given by the father?

    Ans : Same method as in Problem (5)

11. Originally Shyam scored 8 marks more than Ram in Science. But, when 12 marks were added to both later, their ratio became 10 : 9. What were their original marks?

    Ans : See problem (1). Same method.

12. A sum of Rs.60 is divided into 2 parts such that $\frac{3}{10}$ of the 1st part is Rs.4 more than the $\frac{2}{5}$ of the 2nd part. How was the money divided?

Ans : Rs.60 (A)

(B) $\underset{10}{\overset{I}{3}}$ $\underset{5}{\overset{II}{2}}$ (D)
(C) 10   5 (E)
(F) 4

$$\text{1st part} = \frac{A \times C \times D + C \times E \times F}{B \times E + C \times D} = \frac{60 \times 10 \times 2 + 10 \times 5 \times 4}{15 + 20}$$

$$= \frac{1200 + 200}{35} = \frac{1400}{35} = \text{Rs.40}$$

∴ II part = Rs.20

We can get the II part directly by

$$\frac{A \times E \times B - C \times E \times F}{B \times E + C \times D} = \frac{60 \times 5 \times 3 - 10 \times 5 \times 4}{35}$$

$$\frac{900 - 200}{35} = \frac{700}{35} = \text{Rs.20}$$

13. A sum of Rs.110 is divided between A and B such that half of A's share equals $\frac{3}{5}$ of B's share. What are the amounts with A and B?

Ans : A:B Reverse fraction and equate $\frac{2}{1} : \frac{5}{3} = 6 : 5$

So A has Rs.60 and B has Rs.50 (or) if you write $\frac{1}{2} : \frac{3}{5}$ (A first) you get ratio B:A by $1 \times 5 : 2 \times 3 = 5 : 6$

14. B has Rs.50 more than A. A gives 12% of his amount to B, and B gives 5% of his amount to A. Now B has Rs.94 more than A. How much money they had in the beginning?

Ans : (Diff) $\frac{94 - 50}{2} = \frac{44}{2} = 22$

multiply by 100 = 2200

Add 5 × 50 = 250

           = Rs.2450

Divide this by (12 − 5)   = 7 to get A's money.

$$A's = \frac{2450}{7} = \text{Rs.350 and B had Rs.400}$$

15. Peter has Rs.32 more than John. When Peter gives Rs.20 to John, the ratio of money with John and Peter is 17:15. How much money each had in the beginning?

Ans. J   P
           32 more ⎤
           20 deduct ⎦ difference 12
     17 : 15

John's amount $= \dfrac{(15 \times 20) - (12 \times 17)}{17 - 15}$

$= \dfrac{300 - 204}{2} = \dfrac{96}{2} =$ Rs. 48 and

Peter's = Rs.80

16. Same problem as above. Peter gives Rs.40 to John and the new ratio J:P is 11:5

Ans: J   P
           32 more ⎫ difference 8
           40 deduct ⎭
     11 : 5

John's amount $= \dfrac{5 \times 40 - (11 \times -8)}{11 - 5} = \dfrac{200 - (-88)}{6}$

$= \dfrac{288}{6} =$ Rs. 48. So Peter had Rs.80

17. Peter had Rs.32 more than John. When Peter gave Rs.32 to John, the ratio of cash with John and Peter became 5:3. How much they had in the beginning?

Ans: J   P
           32 more ⎫ difference NIL
           32 deduct ⎭
     5 : 3

John had $\dfrac{3 \times 32 + 5 \times 0}{5 - 3} = \dfrac{96}{2} =$ Rs.48

So Peter had Rs.80

18. B had 100 Rupees more than A. A gave 15% of his amount to B and B gave 20% of his amount to A. Now A has Rs.30 more than B. How much each had in the beginning?

Ans : (Difference) $\dfrac{100+30}{2}$ (since A has more money now,

and not B) x 100 = Rs. 6500
Deduct 20 x 100 = Rs. 2000
            Rs. 4500

Divide this by (20 – 15) = 5

A had $\dfrac{4500}{5}$ = Rs.900 & so B had Rs.1000

Note : If we take 15 × 100 we get B's amount direct

Pl. see problem (14)

19. B had Rs.100 more than A. After B gave 15% of his amount to A and A gave 12% of his amount to B, B had Rs.16 more than A. What were the amounts held by them earlier?

Ans : Difference $\dfrac{100-16}{2}$ x 100 = $\dfrac{84}{2}$ x 100 = Rs. 4200
Deduct 15 x 100   = Rs. 1500
                                                Rs. 2700

Divide this by (15 – 12) = 3

A's amount = $\dfrac{2700}{3}$ = Rs.900 So B had Rs.1000

If we take 12 × 100, we get B's amount directly.

See problems 14, 18

20. B had Rs.400 more than A. After B gave 40% of his amount to A and A gave 10% of his amount to B, A had Rs.400 more than B. What were the amounts held by them earlier?

Ans : (Difference) $\dfrac{400+400}{2}$ (since A has more money now and

not B) x 100 = Rs. 40000
Deduct 40 x 400 = Rs. 16000
               Rs. 24000

Divide this by (40 – 10) = 30

So A's amount $\dfrac{24000}{30}$ = Rs.800.   B had Rs.1200

If we take 10 × 400, we get B's amount directly.

Note : Also

A:- (40 – 10)% of A's amount + 40% of 400 is equal to

$\dfrac{400 + 400}{2} = 400$

∴ 30% of A's amount = 400 – 160 = Rs.240

A's amount = $\dfrac{240 \times 100}{30}$ = Rs.800

Thirdly 30% of B's amount = 400 – 10% of 400 = 360

B's amount = 360 × 100 = Rs.1200

❋ ❋ ❋

AGES

1. The total age of a father and son now is 50 years. After 10 years their ages will be in ratio 5:2. What are their ages now?

    Ans : After 10 years, their total age will be 50 + 20 = 70 years in ratio 5:2 ie 50 and 20 years. Now the ages are 40 years & 10 years.

2. The present total age of a husband and wife is 77 years. 7 years ago the ratio of their ages was 5:4. What were their ages then?

    Ans : $77 - (2 \times 7) = 63$ in ratio 5:4

    Husband = 35 years and Wife = 28 years

3. The present ages of Ram and Gopal are in Ratio 3:1. After 6 years, the ratio will be 12:5. What are their ages now?

    Ans : (A) 3:1 (B) (C) 12:5 (D) Time 6 years (E)

    $$\frac{\text{Difference between C and D} \times E}{A \times D \sim B \times C}$$

    $= \dfrac{7 \times 6}{3} = 14$ times of 3:1 = 42 years and 14 years now.

    Ages after 6 years can be got directly by $\dfrac{(3-1) \times 6}{3}$

    = 4 times of 12:5 = 48 years and 20 years or

    by (42 + 6) and (14 + 6)

4. John is 14 years older than Jim. After 10 years their ages will be in ratio 5:3. What are their ages now?

    Ans : $\dfrac{\text{Difference in age}}{\text{Difference in ratio}} \times \text{Ratio}$

    $= \dfrac{14}{2} \times 5:3 = 35$ years and 21 years

    Their ages now = 25 years and 11 years

5. 10 years before, the ages of mother and daughter were in the ratio 3:1. In another 10 years from now the ratio will be 13:7. What are their present ages?

    Ans : Time difference is 20 years.

    Ages 10 years before is got by $\dfrac{20 \times (13 - 7)}{3 \times 7 \sim 13 \times 1}, = \dfrac{20 \times 6}{8} = 15$

    15 times of 3:1 = 45 years and 15 years

    Their present ages = 55 years and 25 years

6. At present, the father's age is 9 times that of the son. After 15 years, he will be thrice as old as his son. What are their ages now?

   Ans : It is 9:1 now and after 15 years 3:1

   See problem (3)
   $$\frac{15 \times (3-1)}{9 \times 1 - 3 \times 1} = \frac{30}{6} = 5 \text{ times of } 9:1$$

   Father's and son's ages now = 45 years, 5 years.

   Their ages after 15 years is got directly by
   $$\frac{15 \times (9-1)}{6} = \frac{120}{6} = 20 \text{ times of } 3:1 = 60 \text{ years \& } 20 \text{ years.}$$

7. The ages of Latha and Sudha are in ratio 5:4. 6 years before, their total age was 42 years. What are their ages now?

   Ans : Now their total ages are 42 + (2 × 6) = 54 years.

   In ratio 5:4 Latha's age = 30 years and

   Sudha's age = 24 years.

8. Now Gupta is 8 years older than Ravi (or, the latter is 8 years younger than the former). After 4 years, 3 times of Gupta's age will be equal to 5 times of Ravi's age. What are their ages now?

   Ans : Even after 4 years, Gupta will be 8 years older than Ravi, so

   Gupta's age after 4 years $= \dfrac{5 \times 8}{5-3} = \dfrac{40}{2} = 20$ years

   Present Age of Gupta $= 16$ and that of Ravi $= 8$

9. At present Vasu is 8 years younger than Gopu (or Gopu is 8 years older than Vasu). 2 years before, 7 times of Vasu's age was equal to 3 times of Gopu's age. What are their present ages?

   Ans : Even 2 years before, Gopu was 8 years older than Vasu. So,

   Gopu's age 2 years before $= \dfrac{7 \times 8}{7-3} = 14$ years and that of

   Vasu = 6

   Their ages now = Gopu = 16 years & Vasu = 8 years.

10. The father's and son's ages are now 30 years and 6 years. After how many years the father's age will be $2\dfrac{1}{2}$ times of the son's age?

Ans: $2\frac{1}{2}$ times is $\frac{5}{2}$ times. Ratio 5:2. The difference of 24 years between them will be the same later too.

So, the ages in future are $\frac{24}{5-2}$ = 8 times of 5:2

= 40 years and 16 years, that is after 10 years.

Note: Same method to find out the ages 'before'.

11. Anil's age now is $2\frac{1}{2}$ times of Gopal's age. After 8 years, Anil's age will be the total of present ages of Anil and Gopal. What are their ages now?

Ans: In another 8 years Anil will be 8 years older, and to get the present total age of Anil + Gopal, the present age of Gopal must be 8 years. Given ratio is $2\frac{1}{2}$:1 or 5:2

Their ages = Anil : Gopal = 20 years : 8 years

12. The present ages of Latha and Jaya are in the ratio 1:4. After 9 years, their total ages will be 11 times the present age of Latha. What are their present ages?

Ans:
	Latha	Jaya
	(A) 1	4(B)
	(D) +9	+9(C)
	(E) 11 times	

now $\frac{C+D}{E \times A - (A+B)} = \frac{18}{11-5}$ = 3 times of 1:4

Their ages now are 3 × 1 = 3 (Latha) and 3 × 4 = 12 (Jaya.)

13. The present ages of Balu and Mohan are in ratio 2:3. 6 years before, Balu's age was $\frac{1}{4}$ of the total of their present age. What are their ages?

Ans: (It is the same as saying that their total age at present is 4 times that of Balu, 6 years before)

$\frac{4 \times 6}{4 \times 2 - (3+2)} = \frac{24}{3}$ = 8 times, of 2:3

Now Balu = 16 years and Mohan = 24 years.

14. **Ages of A and B are in ratio 7:8. The present age of A is equal to the total age of A and B, 12 years before. What are their ages now?**

    Ans : A's age now is equal to total age of A+B; 12 years before, means B's age then was 12 years. Now it is 24 years.

    A:B = X:24 = 7:8. So A's age = 21 years.

15. **The total age of A and B together now, will be double the age of A's after 4 years. If the ratio of their ages after 4 years will be 5:9, what are their ages now?**

    Ans : (Total age difference) = $\dfrac{4+4}{(5+9)-2\times 5} = \dfrac{8}{4}$

    = 2 times of 5:9

    = 10 years and 18 years after 4 years.

    Now A:B = 6 years and 14 years.

16. **The total age of P and R together now is 3 times R's age 5 years before. If the ratio of their ages 5 years before was 4:3, what are their present ages?**

    Ans : (Total age difference) $\dfrac{5+5}{(4+3)\sim 3\times 3} = \dfrac{10}{2} = 5$.

    5 times 4 : 3 = 20 years and 15 years before 5 years.

    Now P : R = 25 years and 20 years.

17. **A's age after 12 years will be equal to the ages of A and B together now. If after 12 years the ages will be in ratio 5:4, what are their ages now?**

    Ans : If after 12 years A's age will be equal to the present ages of A & B together, then B's present age must be 12 and after 12 years, it will be 24 years.

    And so, 5 : 4 = X : 24 = future age of A will be 30.

    His present age is (30 − 12) = 18 years.

18. **10 years before, the ratio of the ages of A:B was 1:3 and B's age then was half of their ages together now. What are their ages?**

    Ans: (Total age difference) $\dfrac{20}{2\times 3 \sim (3+1)} = \dfrac{20}{2} = 10$.

    10 times of 1:3 = 10 years and 30 years 10 years before.

    Now it is A:B = 20 years and 40 years.

PROFIT AND LOSS

1. A fruiterer bought some apples at Rs.2 each and thrice of that quantity at Rs.3 each and sold each apple at Rs.3.50 and made a profit of Rs.66. How many apples of each variety was bought?

   Ans: Profit on I & II variety = Rs. $1\frac{1}{2} : \frac{1}{2}$

   Quantity bought ratio = 1 : 3

   Profit amount = $1\frac{1}{2} \times 1 + 3 \times \frac{1}{2} = 1\frac{1}{2} + 1\frac{1}{2} =$ Rs.3

   Quantity bought $\frac{66}{3} \times (1:3) =$ 22 apples at Rs.2 and 66 apples at Rs.3

2. A and B invested Rs.4500 and Rs.7500 in a business. At the end of the year, after paying A's salary from profits, the balance was divided according to the ratio of their capital. If A & B got Rs.700 and Rs.750 respectively, what was A's salary?

   Ans: Ratio of capital = 3:5 or 9:15.

   Final ratio of profit = 14:15 (each unit Rs.50)

   A got 5 units more (14-9), that is 5×50 = Rs.250 which is his salary.

3. A puts Rs.2500 in business for 6 months and B, his partner puts Rs.1250 and gets $\frac{2}{5}$ of the whole profit. For how many months did B keep his capital in business?

   Ans: Capital ratio = 2:1, profit ratio = $\frac{3}{5} : \frac{2}{5}$ (or) 3:2.

   Investment time of A is known, make it common.

   Capital ratio = 6:3, profit ratio 6:4.

   ∴ Time of investment A:B = 3:4.

   Since A's time is 6 months, B's time is 8 months.

4. A and B start business with Rs.6000 and Rs.8000 respectively. After some time B adds Rs.3000 to his capital and gets Rs.2500, out of the total profit of Rs.4000 at the end of the year. When did B increase his capital?

Ans : Initial capital ratio of A : B = 3 : 4   (1)
Later capital ratio of A : B = 6 : 11   (2)
Profit ratio of   A : B = 3 : 5   (3)
As there is no change in A's capital make it common

```
        A     B      C  P  C
(1)     6  :  8      8  10 11
(2)     6  :  11
(3)     6  :  10
```

Investment time ratio = (11–10):(10–8) = 1:2 for the year.
                          first

That is A 4 months and B 8 months. So B increased his capital after 4 months.

5. P and R start business with Rs.400 and Rs.600 respectively. After some time, P adds Rs.200 to his capital. After another 10 months, the profit was Rs.150, out of which R got Rs.80. When did P increase his capital?

Ans :   P   R

1. Original investment ratio = 2 : 3
2. Later investment ratio   = 1 : 1 (10 months investment)
3. Profit ratio   = 70 : 80 (or) 7 : 8

Make R common as his investment did not change.

```
         P     R
1.  =   16  :  24
2.  =   24  :  24    10 months
3.  =   21  :  24    16  21  24
```

Ratio of time investment for P = (24 – 21) : (21 – 16) = 3:5
The latter part was 10 months. So the former part is 6.
That is P increased his capital after 6 months.

Note : If A = 16, B = 24 and C = 21 and D = 10 months

then $\dfrac{(B-C) \times D}{C - A} = \dfrac{30}{5} = 6$ months after.

6. A and B invest Rs.2400 and Rs.3000 respectively in a business. B draws salary from profit and the balance is divided between them in the ratio of their capital. If A gets Rs.480 and total profit is Rs.1280, what is B's salary?

Ans : Capital ratio of A : B = 4:5.

So, if A got Rs.480, B should get $\frac{480}{4} \times 5$ = Rs.600.

But he got Rs.(1280 – 480) = Rs.800.

So his salary is Rs.200 [see problem (2). There if B got Rs.750, A should get $\frac{750}{5} \times 3$ = Rs.450. But he got Rs.700. So, his salary is Rs.250]

7. **P and R have capitals of Rs.1750 and Rs.2750 in business. Manager P gets his salary of 10% of profit and the balance is divided in the ratio of investments. If R's share is Rs.330, how much did P get?**

   Ans : Ratio of Investment = 7:11.

   So if R gets Rs.330, P's share is $\frac{330}{11} \times 7$ = Rs.210.

   Total divisible profit = 210 + 330 = Rs.540.

   P's salary is 10% of profit. So, 90% of profit = Rs.540.

   Total profit = $\frac{540 \times 100}{90}$ = Rs.600

   Totally P got Rs.210+10% of 600 = Rs.270.

   <u>Another method:</u> Balance 90 in ratio 7:11 gives 35:55.

   Total P:R = (35 + 10) : 55 = 9:11

   So, if R gets Rs.330, P gets a total of $\frac{330 \times 9}{11}$ = <u>Rs.270</u>

8. **Ram and Gopal invest money in business and by the year end earn profit amounting to 15% of the total capital. Ram, whose capital was Rs.2100, got $\frac{3}{8}$ of the profit. Find Gopal's share?**

   Ans : If Ram got $\frac{3}{8}$ of profit, it means their capitals are in ratio $\frac{3}{8}$ and $\frac{5}{8}$ = 3 : 5. So Gopal's capital is $\frac{2100}{3} \times 5$ = Rs.3500 and his share is 15% of it = <u>Rs.525</u>

9. **The cash with P and R was in ratio 3:5. They spend Rs.60 and Rs.70 respectively and now the amount left with them is in ratio 1:2. How much money they had in the beginning?**

Ans : New ratio 1 : 2 (A:B) Amount spent 60 ; 70 (C,D) Old ratio 3 : 5 (E,F)

$$\frac{(\sim) \text{ Diff between A} \times \text{D and B} \times \text{C}}{(\sim) \text{ Diff between A} \times \text{F and B} \times \text{E}} = \frac{120-70}{6-5} = 50 \text{ times.}$$

So, amount with them was

$50 \times 3 : 5 = $ Rs.150(P) & Rs.250 (R)

10. Jim and John invest together Rs.5000. Jim withdraws his amount after 6 months. 10 months thereafter, profits were shared according to the ratio of their capital and Jim and John got Rs.350 and Rs.400 respectively. How much each invested?

	Jim	John
Ans : Profit ratio	7 :	8 (or) 21 : 24
Time ratio	3 :	8 (∴ 6 months and 16 months)

    Capital ratio $= \dfrac{21}{3} : \dfrac{24}{8} = 7 : 3$

    The capital of Jim $= 5000 \times \dfrac{7}{10} =$ Rs.3500 and

    John's capital = Rs.1500

11. A invests Rs.2100 and after 5 months, B joins him with some capital. At the year end, the profits received by them were Rs.240 and Rs.360 respectively. How much capital did B put in?

    Ans : Profit ratio = 2:3, Time ratio = 12:7 (B came 5 months later)

    Capital ratio $= \dfrac{2}{12} : \dfrac{3}{7} = \dfrac{14:36}{84}$ or 7:18

    So B's capital $= \dfrac{2100}{7} \times 18 =$ Rs.5400

12. P and R start a business with capitals Rs.2500 and Rs.3750 respectively. They take 10% and 15% respectively of profits towards their salaries, and then divide the balance profit according to the ratio of their capitals. If P got Rs.600 how much did R get out of the whole profit?

Ans :   P : R
Invested ratio = 2 : 3
    Salaries   = 2 : 3 same as invested ratio

So profits shared by them including their salaries are in ratio 2:3

P got Rs.600 So, R's share = $\dfrac{600}{2} \times 3$ = Rs.900

[suppose their salaries are 10% and 20% (P:R) and P gets Rs.570 what is R's share?]

Ans :   P   R
Capital   2 :   3
Salary   10 :   20 (balance 70)

Profit = $\dfrac{70 \times 2}{5} + \dfrac{70 \times 3}{5} = 28 + 42$

Total is (profit + salaries) 38 and 62 or 19 : 31.

P gets Rs.570. So R gets total $\dfrac{570}{19} \times 31$ = Rs.930

This also gives total profit as Rs.1500

13. **A, B and C start a business with Rs.14000, Rs.7000 and Rs.3500 respectively. A and B receive 20% and 10% respectively of the profits towards their salaries. Balance profit is divided according to the ratio of their capital. If C gets at the year end a sum of Rs.1020, how much A and B get?**

Ans :   A : B : C
Capital ratio = 4 : 2 : 1
    Salary   = 20 : 10 : - (balance 70)
                +   +   +

Profit share $\dfrac{70 \times 4}{7}$ $\dfrac{70 \times 2}{7}$ $\dfrac{70 \times 1}{7}$

= (20+40), (10+20), (10)
=   6   :   3   :   1 ratio

C got Rs.1020.

So A gets 3 × 1020 = Rs.3060 and B gets 6 × 1020 = Rs.6120

14. Salaries of A and B are in ratio 7 : 5. Another sum of arrears of Rs.400 was distributed to both and now A has Rs.100 more, than the excess amount he had in the beginning. If A has $\frac{19}{13}$ times the money that B has, how much money they had in the beginning?

Ans : Find out the Number of times of the ratio 7 : 5

For Numerator

$(19 + 13) 100 - (19 - 13) 400 = 3200 - 2400 = 800$

For Denominator

7 : 5

19 : 13 Cross multiply, find the difference and multiply it by 2

$[(7 \times 13) \sim (19 \times 5)] = 2(95 - 91) = \underline{8}$

$\frac{800}{8} = 100$ times.

The amount they had in the beginning =

A = 100×7 = Rs.700 and B = 100×5 = Rs.500.

❈ ❈ ❈

MISC

1. A man engaged a clerk on condition that he would pay him Rs.6000 and a briefcase after one year of completion of service. But, the clerk left after seven months and received the briefcase and cash Rs.3,375. What is the cost of the briefcase?

    Ans : For 7 months the clerk should get 7×500

    $$= Rs.3500 + \frac{7}{12} \text{ cost of Briefcase.}$$

    He got Rs.125 less which is equal to the $\frac{5}{12}$ cost of Briefcase.

    Cost of Briefcase $= \dfrac{125 \times 12}{5} = Rs.300$

2. A house is insured for Rs.85000, so as to cover both the value of house and insurance premium at $2\frac{1}{2}$%. What is the value of the house?

    Ans : Deduct $2\frac{1}{2}$% of $85000 = 85000 - (1700 + 425)$

    $85000 - 2125 = Rs.82875$

3. A dinner party is arranged by a contractor for 21 persons and rate per person is fixed so that he may gain $12\frac{1}{2}$% on his outlay. 3 persons were absent and rest paid at fixed price. So, the contractor lost Rs.4. What was the fixed charge per person?

    Ans : Total persons 21. Attended 18. Loss Rs.4 and profit $12\frac{1}{2}$%, which means if C.P = 8 fixed price is 9

    Cost $= 21 \times 8 = Rs.168.$

    Collected amound is $18 \times 9 = Rs.162$

    So loss is Rs.6. If loss is Rs.6 - fixed price is Rs.9.

    For loss of Rs.4 - fixed price $= \dfrac{9}{6} \times 4 = Rs.6$

4. A worker was engaged at Rs.10/- per day, and he agreed with a cut of Rs.5 per day when he was absent. If at the end of 30 days, he received, Rs.240 how many days he worked?

Ans : He should have got Rs.300. He received Rs.60 less. Divide this by (Rs.10 + Rs.5) = 15

$\dfrac{60}{15} = 4$ days he was absent. Worked for 26 days.

5. A train has 26 compartments. Some compartments have seating capacity of 40 passengers, and others 45 passengers. If the train carried 1080 persons how many compartments are there of each kind?

Ans : All compartments took a minimum of 40 passengers i.e. $40 \times 26 = 1040$. Balance 40 was taken by compartments which took each 5 persons more (45 – 40).

So, $\dfrac{40}{5} = 8$ compartments of 45 persons each and 18 compartments of 40 persons each.

6. If each boy is given 3 mangoes, the available stock can be given to a certain number of boys. If each boy is given 5 mangoes then they can be given to 4 boys less. How many mangoes are there?

Ans : Difference in boys (4) $\times \dfrac{\text{product of } 3 \times 5}{\text{Diff in rate } (5-3)} = \dfrac{4 \times 15}{2}$

= 30 Mangoes.

7. In a refugee camp there is enough food for 30 days for 20,000 persons. After 10 days, another 5,000 persons join in. If the ration to each is reduced by $\dfrac{1}{2}$, for how many more days will the food available be sufficient?

Ans : Ignore zeros and reduce old persons to 4 and new persons to 1. After 10 days food is available for 20 days for 4 at full ration. For 5 at $\dfrac{1}{2}$ ration, the food will be sufficient for

$\dfrac{4 \times 20 \times 2}{5} = 32$ days.

8. A radio dealer fixed the S.P of a transistor radio at Rs.144 each at a profit of $12\dfrac{1}{2}$%. 3 transistors broke into pieces and rest were sold at the fixed S.P. If his loss on the whole was Rs.96, how many transistors did he have in the beginning?

Ans : With profit $12\frac{1}{2}\%$, the C.P is $144 \times \frac{8}{9}$ = Rs.128.

Difference of Rs.16 on each article.

Loss on 3 articles broken at S.P rate = 3 × 144 = Rs.432.
Actual loss Rs.96. Apparent loss = 432–96 = Rs.336.

No of transistors = $\frac{336}{16}$ = 21.

9. **The length and breadth of a room are in ratio 5:2. If length had been 8m less and width 4m more, the room would have been a square. What are the measurements of the room?**

   Ans : $\frac{8+4}{5-2}$ times $5:2 = \frac{12}{3}$ = 4 times of 5:2.

   Length = 4 × 5 = 20m   Breadth = 4 × 2 = 8m.

10. **There is a rectangular field. If the length is less by 2m and breadth is more by 5m, the area will be increased by 160 sq.m. If length is 4m more, and breadth 3m less, then the area will be 2 sq.m.less. What is the length and breadth of the field?**

    Ans : Write like this

Length	Breadth	
2	− 5	(2 × 5 + 160) = 170
4	− 3	(4 × 3 − 2) = 10

    Breadth = $\frac{170 \times 3 + 5 \times 10}{5 \times 4 \sim 3 \times 2} = \frac{560}{14}$ = 40m

    Length = $\frac{170 \times 4 + 2 \times 10}{5 \times 4 \sim 3 \times 2} = \frac{700}{14}$ = 50m

11. **In a school the ratio of students in 7th and 8th std., is 4:5. For going on a picnic, each student paid as many paise as there are students in the class. If the total amount collected was Rs.502.25, how many students are there in each class?**

    Ans : Add $4^2 + 5^2$ = 41. Divide 50225 paise by 41 = 1225.

    Its square root = 35

    So, 7th class students = 35 × 4 = 140

    8th class students = 35 × 5 = 175.

12. A chair and a table cost Rs.65 and Rs.140 respectively. If 10 items of these together were bought for Rs.1100 how many chairs and tables were bought?

   Ans : A minimum of Rs.65 was paid on all 10 items = Rs.650. Balance Rs.450 was paid on tables which cost Rs.75 each more. So tables = $\dfrac{450}{75}$ = 6. So chairs = 4.

13. A merchant buys 12kg of one kind of oil at Rs.18 per kilo and some kg of another kind of oil at Rs.20 per kilo and after mixing both sells at Rs.20.40 per kilo. His gain is Rs.36. How much quantity of 2nd variety did he buy? What is the cost price of mixture?

   Ans : Profit on 1st variety is Rs.2.40 on 1kg. On 12kg it is Rs.28.80. Balance profit of Rs.7.20 is got by the profit of 40 paise per Kg on 2nd variety.

   2nd variety quantity = $\dfrac{720}{40}$ = 18 Kg.

   Total quantity is 30kg & Profit is Rs.36

   On 1Kg profit is Rs.1.20. So, Cost price of 1 kg = Rs.19.20

14. In a club there are 2 classes of members who pay Rs.13 and Rs.8 respectively per month. If the collection in a month is Rs.1460 and the total members are 150, how many are there in each class?

   Ans : If all 150 members paid Rs.8 per head, the total is Rs.1200.

   Balance Rs.260 was paid by members,

   who paid (13−8) = Rs.5 more per head.

   So members who paid at Rs.13 = $\dfrac{260}{5}$ = 52

   Rest of 98 paid Rs.8

15. A sum is divided (Rs.1200) into 3 parts such that $\dfrac{1}{2}$ of 1st part, $\dfrac{1}{4}$ of 2nd part and $\dfrac{1}{6}$ of 3rd part are equal. The 3rd part is equal to what?

   Ans : Take the ratio as 2:4:6 (or) 1:2:3

   So 3rd part = $\dfrac{1200 \times 3}{6}$ = Rs.600

Solve the Problems in Short-Cut Methods

16. **In an election contested by 2 candidates, 8% of voters did not vote. Successful candidate won by 8,400 votes, getting 48.4% of votes polled. How many votes were cast for each candidate?**

    Ans : As 8% did not vote, winner (A) got 48.4% of votes and the loser (B) must have got 43.6% of votes. The difference between A and B is 4.8% which is equal to 8,400.

    So total votes = $\dfrac{8,400 \times 100}{4.8}$ = 1,75,000

    A got 48.4% = 84,700 and B got 43.6% = 76,300

17. **In a village the members in Tiger and Lion parties were in ratio 5:2. After 50 persons from the first joined the second, the ratio became 25:24. How many members were there initially in each party?**

    Ans : New ratio is 25:24 (Total 49). Old Ratio 5:2 can be written as 35:14 (Total 49). So if 10 persons cross, Total is 49

    If 50 persons cross, Total = <u>245</u> members.

    Tiger party had <u>175</u> and Lion party had <u>70</u> members.

18. **The total salary of 2 watchmen is Rs.510. One spends 80% of his salary and the other 70%. If their savings are in ratio 3:4, what are their salaries?**

    Ans : Savings should be 20% : 30% or 2:3 or 6:9

    But they are 3:4 or 6:8 left side common

    So, the salaries are in ratio 9:8

    That is $\dfrac{510 \times 9}{17}$ = Rs.270 and $\dfrac{510 \times 8}{17}$ = Rs.240

19. **Cost of 2 articles are in ratio 3:2. On the first there is 40% loss and on the second 30% gain. What is overall percentage of loss?**

    Ans : $\dfrac{(3 \times 40) - (2 \times 30)}{3+2} = \dfrac{120 - 60}{5} = \dfrac{60}{5} = 12\%$.

    Note : The actual cost of articles make no difference to the overall percentage.

20. **In a school, the girls and boys are in ratio 2:3. 60% of girls passed in the examination and if the overall pass was 48%, what was the percentage of pass for boys?**

Ans : $\dfrac{48 \times (2+3) - (2 \times 60)}{3} = \dfrac{240-120}{3} = \dfrac{120}{3} = 40\%$

40% of boys passed.

Note : The total number of students make no difference to the percentage asked.

21. 280 students appeared for an interview, and 50% of girls and $6\dfrac{1}{4}$% of boys were declared successful. If such students are 25% on the whole, how many girls and boys appeared for the interview?

    Ans : Write like this

Girls	Total	Boys
50	25	$6\dfrac{1}{4}$

    Ratio of Girls : Boys = $(25 - 6\dfrac{1}{4}) : (50 - 25) = 18\dfrac{3}{4} : 25$

    $\qquad = 75 : 100 = 3 : 4$

    That is Girls 120 and Boys 160.

    General Note : Suitable changes are to be made in percentages according to the data given.

    Ex.: 75% failed means 25% passed. 3/5 passed means 2/5 failed, and so on.

22. The total salary drawn by 3 watchmen, A, B and C is Rs.1720. They spend 70%, 60% and 50% respectively from their salaries. If the balances with them are in ratio 1:2:3, what is the salary of each?

    Ans : Balances to be 30%, 40%, 50% or 3:4:5

    Actual Ratio   :   1 : 2 : 3
    To be Ratio   :   3 : 4 : 5

    Write in 2 pairs as shown and cross multiply.

    A   B   B   C
    1   2   2   3   start from left top
    3   4   4   5
    (1 × 4) : (2 × 3)   (2 × 5) : (3 × 4)
    =   4 : 6   10 : 12

or 2 : 3   or   5 : 6

Make B common. So ratio 10:15:18

Salary of A = $\dfrac{1720 \times 10}{43}$ = Rs.400

Salary of B = Rs.600

Salary of C = Rs.720

23. **A student who got 38% of marks in an examination failed short of 26 marks. If he had scored 44% of marks, he would have got 13 marks more than minimum pass marks. What is the minimum pass percentage?**

   Ans : Difference between 44% and 38% is 6%.

   Difference between (–26) and (+13) is 39 marks.

   $\dfrac{39}{6}$ is 6.5 (ie) total marks of the exam is $6\dfrac{1}{2}$ hundreds or 650 marks.

   Now 44% of 650 is $\dfrac{650 \times 44}{100}$ = 286 which is 13 more.

   So to pass he should get $\dfrac{273}{650}$ (or) $\dfrac{21}{50} \times 100$ = 42%.

   Also Note: The difference in marks can be written in ratio left hand side: right hand side as 26:13 or 2:1 or 4:2 or 6:3 etc. Now (38+left hand side) must be equal to (44 - right hand side).

   Here 4 : 2 satisfies 38 + 4 = 44 – 2 = 42%.

❋ ❋ ❋

AVERAGES

1. **What is the average of the first five odd natural numbers?**

   Ans : When consecutive odd numbers are taken it is always the middle number, that is Average.

   In this case it is 5.

   In fact, when any odd consecutive numbers are taken it is always the middle number that is average.

   Ex : 8,9,10,11,12,13,14 - average is 11.

   or 10,12,14,16,18 - average 14

   It will be seen also that $\frac{8+14}{2} = 11$ & $\frac{18+10}{2} = 14$

2. **What is the average of 110, 111, 112, 113 (4 consecutive numbers)**

   Ans : The average $\frac{113+110}{2} = \frac{223}{2} = 111.5$

3. **The average age of a class of 30 students is 18. When the teacher's age is included the average becomes 19. What is the age of the teacher?**

   Ans : Teacher's age is (30 + 19) = 49 years.

4. **Last year the average salary of 24 employees in a factory was Rs.800. This year 10 of them got promoted and their salary increased at an average of Rs.24. What is the average of all the employees now?**

   Ans : The increase of 24 × 10 = Rs.240 is spread over all the 24 members at Rs.10 per person.

   New average 800 + 10 = Rs.810.

5. **There are 5 numbers. The average of first four is 8 and the last four is 10. If the 1st number is 4, what is the last number?**

   Ans : 4 × 10 – 4 × 8 = 8. The aggregate of last four is more and the last Number is 8 + 4 = 12.

6. **There are 7 numbers. The average of first six is 9 and the average of last six is 10. If the last number is 11, what is the first number?**

   Ans : 6 × 10 – 6 × 9 = 6. The aggregate of first six is less. So, the first Number is 11 – 6 = 5.

SURA'S ❈ Solve the Problems in Short-Cut Methods

7. There are 4 numbers whose total is 26. The average of first 3 numbers is 5, and the average of last three is 7. If the second number is 9, what is the 3rd number?

    Ans : (3 × 5 + 3 × 7) – 26 = 10. Third number = 10 – 9 = 1.

8. Babu has 10 marbles more than the average of marbles with Babu and Somu put together. If Somu has 20 marbles, how many does Babu have?

    Ans : Simply add 10 + 20 = 30 which is the average of both. So both have 2 × 30 = 60 and so Babu has 40.

9. If 8 students are seated on each bench, 3 benches are left over. If 5 students are seated on each bench, 12 students are left over. How many benches and students are there?

    Ans : $\dfrac{(8 \times 3) + 12}{8 - 5}$ = 12 benches, So, students are (12 × 5) + 12 = 72

10. A student bought 5 books at Rs.2 each, 4 books at Rs.5 each and some more books at Rs.6 each. If the average cost of all books was Rs.4, how many books of Rs.6 each did he buy?

    Ans : Take Rs.4. Value difference 5 × (2 – 4) + 4 × (5 – 4)
    = –10 + 4 = Rs. –6.

    This difference is spread over on books which cost Rs.2 more than the overall average.

    So $\dfrac{6}{2}$ = 3 books of Rs.6 each was bought.

11. There are 4 numbers. The average of the first 3 numbers is 2 less than the average of the last 3 numbers. If the first number is 8, what is the last number?

    Ans : The difference is 3 × 2 = 6. The second aggregate is more. So, last number = 8 + 6 = 14.

12. The average of 9 consecutive odd numbers is 11. What is the difference between the first and the last number?

    Ans : (9 – 1) × 2 = 16 (Difference between 2 consecutive numbers is 2)

13. The average of 5 consecutive even numbers is 12. What is the difference between the first and the last number?

Ans : (5 – 1) × 2 = 8

(Difference between 2 consecutive Numbers is 2).

For problems (12) & (13) we have not used the given average for working. The formula used is

Last number
= 1st number + (no.of terms –1) × Common difference.

14. To pass the examination a student must get an average of 35% marks on the aggregate. If a student got 56 marks for 150 in 1st paper, 75 marks for 150 in the II paper, what percentage he should score in the third paper set for 200 marks?

Ans :   To pass he must get 5 × 35   = 175 marks.

Got in 2 papers for 300 marks = 131 marks.

To get balance 44 marks out of 200 he should score 22%

15. The average marks of a class of 40 students was 29.5. Then the marks of 3 students were changed from 50 to 40, 60 to 55 and from 31 to 50. What is the new average of the class?

Ans :   The difference in marks –10, –5, and +19 that is +4 marks is spread over 40 students.

$$\frac{4}{40} = \frac{1}{10} = 0.1$$

New Average = 29.5 + 0.1 = 29.6

16. In a class, the average marks of all was 50. Out of the students, 5 got each '0' marks. If they had not gone for examination, the class average would have increased by 10 marks. How many students are there in the class?

Ans :   The class average applies to 5 students also who got zero.
5 × 50 = 250 marks.

Divide this by the increase in average $\frac{250}{10}$ = 25 students. This excludes the 5 above.

Total students = 25 + 5 = 30

In Notation: If A = 50; B = 5, C = 0, D = 10 then

$$\frac{B \times (A - C)}{D} + B.$$

17. In a class the average marks of all students was 50(A). Out of them 5(B) got each zero marks (C) and another 5(D) got an average of 32 marks (E). If these 10 students had not gone for the examination the class average would have increased by 17 marks (F). How many students are there in the class?

Ans : The increase in average is caused by removal of these marks:

5 (who got zero each) × 50 (class average) = 250

5 (who got average 32) × 18 (Difference between 50 and 32) = 90

$$250 + 90 = 340$$

To get the number of students, divide this by increase in average $\dfrac{340}{17} = 20$. But this is exclusive of the above 10 students. So Total no. of students in the class = 20 + 10 = 30

In Notation: $\left[\dfrac{B(A-C)+D(A-E)}{F} \right] + (B+D)$

18. The average marks of a class in VIII Std examination was 50 marks. Out of the students, 5 had an average of 60 marks. If they were not in the class, the new average would have been less by 2 marks. How many students are there in the class?

Ans : The class average applies to the 5 students also who got an average of 60 marks.

The difference of average 10 marks. = 5 × 10 = 50 marks.

Because of the removal of these marks the average fell by 2 marks. So, the students are $\dfrac{50}{2} = 25$, which is exclusive of 5 students.

Total strength of class = 25 + 5 = 30

In Notation: A = 50; B = 5; C = 60; D = 2

then $\dfrac{B(A \sim C)}{D} + B$ (~ means deduct lower figure from higher figure)

19. The average marks of all students in VI std is 50, and if 10 students whose average is 30 marks, leave the class, the new average increases by 10 marks.

How many students are there in the class?

Ans : The class average applies to 10 students also who have an average of 30. Total difference = 10(50 − 30) = 200 marks.

No. of Students = $\frac{200}{10}$ (increase in marks average) + 10 (who left)

= 20 + 10 = 30.

See problem (16) words like 'leave the class' or 'did not write the exam' etc mean the same.

20. The class' average marks was 50. Out of them 20 got an average of 44 marks and the average of the rest was 60 marks. How many students are there in the class?

Ans : Fall in average (50 − 44) for 20 students is a total difference of 120 marks. This got spread over the students who got (60 − 50) = 10 marks average more.

∴ Students $\frac{120}{10}$ = 12 which excludes the above 20

So Total no. of students = 12 + 20 = 32

21. The average income of 30 persons is Rs.180. 10 more persons join the group and the overall average increases to Rs.190. What is the average income of the new entrants?

Ans : Total no. of persons 40. Increase in average is Rs.10.

New entrants = 10. Old average = Rs.180

∴ Average of new entrants = $180 + \frac{40 \times 10 \text{ (Increase)}}{10 \text{ (Persons)}}$

= Rs.220

A = 30; B = Rs.180; C = 10 extra persons. D = 190

New average for all = $\frac{B^1 + (A+C)(D-B)}{C}$

22. The average marks in Maths of a class of 70 students is 65. Out of them 2 got zero marks, 2 got 100 marks each and 16 others' average was 50 marks. What is the average of the remaining students?

Ans : As an average, the difference in marks 16(65 − 50) + 2(65 − 0) − 2(100 − 65) is spread over the remaining 50 students. So, their average is:

$\frac{240 + 130 - 70}{50} = \frac{300}{50}$ = + 6 marks increase.

So, their average = 65 + 6 = 71 marks.

23. Class' average 50 marks (A); out of them 10(B) have average 70(C). If they were not in class, the average will fall by 10 marks (D). How many students are there?

Ans : $\dfrac{B(C-A)}{D} + B = \dfrac{200}{10} + 10 = 30$ students.

24. The class' average mark was 50. When, 5 students who got zero, and 5 who got an average of 35 marks and another 5 who had an average of 46 marks joined the class, the class average fell by $7\dfrac{2}{3}$ marks. How many students are there now?

Ans : Total Difference $5(50-0) + 5(50-35) + 5(50-46) =$
$$250 + 75 + 20 = 345 \text{ Marks.}$$

Divide this by fall in marks.

$$\dfrac{345 \times 3}{23} = 45$$

Students now = 45. Previously it was 30.

25. If in the above problem these 15 students leave the class and thereby the class average increases by 23 marks then,

Ans : $\dfrac{345}{23} = 15$ excluding these 15 students.

So total nos. in class = <u>30</u>

26. Money was collected from 10 persons for a building fund. 7 persons paid Rs.500 each and the rest three paid Rs.150, Rs.250 and Rs.300 respectively, more than the average amount paid by all. What is the average? What is the amount collected?

Ans : Total extra amount = (150 + 250 + 300) = Rs.700

Spread this over the 7 persons whose payment is known.

$$\dfrac{700}{7} = \text{Rs.100}$$

Average of all = Rs.500 + Rs.100 = Rs.600

Amount collected = Rs.6000

27. Rama's salary is Rs.1500 and Gopal's salary is Rs.2400 and Sarma's salary is Rs.300 more than the average of all three. What is their average? What is Sarma's salary?

Ans : Add all amounts and divide by 2.

$$= \dfrac{1500 + 2400 + 300}{2} = \dfrac{4200}{2} = \text{Rs. 2100 average of all 3}$$

Sarma's salary = 2100 + 300 = Rs.2400.

28. 8 persons gave donation to a fund. Out of them 5 paid an average of Rs.35. The rest three paid Rs.15, Rs.18 and Rs.12 respectively, more than the average amount paid by all the 8 persons. What is their average?

   Ans : Amount paid more by the 3 = Rs.45.
   Spread this over 5 persons whose average is known $\frac{45}{5}$ = Rs.9
   Average of all = 35 + 9 = <u>Rs.44</u>.

29. The average salary of 10 clerks and Manager of a firm was Rs.90. The manager, whose salary was Rs.300 left and another Manager came in his place. The average salary of all now came to Rs.85. What is the salary of the new Manager?

   Ans : Total fall in amount = 11 (90 − 85) = Rs.55.
   New Manager's salary = 300 − 55 = <u>Rs.245</u>.

30. 160 students paid an average of Rs.5, towards a fund and when another 40 students also paid for the fund, the average for all became Rs.5.20. What was the average amount paid by the 40 students?

   Ans : Difference of 20 paise on (160 + 40) = 200 students is due to the extra amount paid by the 40 students.
   $\frac{1}{5} \times \frac{200}{40}$ = Re.1 So 40 students average = Rs.5 + 1 = Rs.6

31. 36 students pay Rs.2.50 each for a party and after some students who did not pay also join them, the average fell to Rs.1.80. How many more students joined?

   Ans : Difference in amount is 70 paise or
   $$\frac{Rs.\frac{7}{10} \times 36}{\frac{180}{100}} = 7 \times \frac{36}{10} \times \frac{5}{9} = 14.$$ Another 14 joined.

32. A trader buys 32 suitcases at Rs.300 each and 28 briefcases at Rs.225 each. What is the average cost of an article?

   Ans : Cost 300 : 225 = 4 : 3 (75 times reduced)
   Items: 32 : 28 = 8 : 7
   average $\frac{75(8 \times 4 + 7 \times 3)}{8 + 7} = \frac{75 \times 53}{15}$ = Rs.265 average cost.

Solve the Problems in Short-Cut Methods

33. The average height of a class was 155cm. There were 20 boys and 10 girls, and the average height of a girl was 15cm less than average height of the boys. What was the height of the boys?

    Ans : Total difference in height of girls = 15 × 10 = 150 cm.

    This is spread over the entire class of 30 students.

    Average = $\dfrac{150}{30}$ = 5 cm So, average height of Boys

    = 155 + 5 = <u>160 cm</u>

34. The average height of 40 students in a class was 160cm. After 10 students joined, the average became 156cm. What is the total height of the 10 students newly joined?

    Ans : If the average height of 10 also was 160cm, 1600cm would have been added without any change in the total average.

    The fall was a total of (40+10) × (160 –156) cm = 200cm.

    So, the total height of 10 new students

    $$= 1600 - 200 = 1400 \text{cm}.$$

35. A batsman's average was 20 runs. In another 2 innings he scored 0, and 10 runs, and his average became 15 runs. How many innings did he play?

    Ans: Average of 15 runs is applicable to the last innings too.

    Difference is 2 × 15 – (0 + 10) = 30 – 10 = 20 runs.

    The difference between old and new average

    $$= 20 - 15 = 5 \text{ runs}.$$

    Innings played previously = $\dfrac{20}{5}$ = 4.

    Total innings <u>6</u>

36. 80kg of sugar at Rs.7 per kilo and 120kg of sugar at Rs.6 per kilo were bought. What was the average cost of both?

    Ans : Quantity Ratio = 80:120 = 2:3

    $$2 \times 7 + \dfrac{3 \times 6}{2+3} = \dfrac{32}{5} = \text{Rs. } 6.40$$

    Note : The actual quantity bought makes no difference, since we have not reduced the cost in ratio.

    Pl. see problem (32).

PERCENTAGES

1. A dealer marks his goods 25% above Cost Price and then while selling gives a discount of 12% on M.P. What is his percentage of Profit?

   Ans : Formula :- $\left[(x-y) = \dfrac{xy}{100}\right]\%$

   $(25 - 12) - 12\%$ of $25 = 13 - 3 = 10\%$ Profit.

2. In the above problem the discount on M.P. is 20%. Profit is

   Ans : Then $(25 - 20) - 20\%$ of $25 = 5 - 5 = 0$ No loss. No gain.

   Note : that a discount of more than 20% on M.P. results in Loss.

3. If M.P. is 10 % above C.P. and discount is 9 % on M.P, profit is

   Ans : Then $(10 - 9) - 9\%$ of $10 = 1 - \dfrac{9}{10} = 0.1\%$ Profit.

4. Selling Price of 12 fruits is equal to the Cost Price of 16 fruits. What is the Profit percentage?

   Ans : $\dfrac{16-12}{12} \times 100 = \dfrac{100}{3} = 33\dfrac{1}{3}\%$ profit.

5. A shop keeper sells 2 radios, each for Rs.600. If he gains 12% on one and suffers a loss of 12% on the other, what is his overall gain or loss?

   Ans : When S.P. is the same and percentage of loss on one is equal to the percentage of gain on the other, then overall it is always, loss.

   % of Loss = $\dfrac{12^2}{10^2} = 1.2^2 = 1.44\%$ Loss.

6. Is it possible to give successive discounts of 80%, 20% and 5%?

   Ans: Yes.

7. Are successive discounts of 20% and 15% equal to the successive discounts of 15% and 20%, or, not?

   Ans: They are equal.

8. A trader buys 2 boxes for the same price. He sells one at 10% loss. If he wants an overall profit of 10%, at what percentage of profit should he sell the 2nd box?

Ans : When buying, prices of 2 boxes are the same.

$$\frac{\text{Profit} - \text{Loss}}{2} = \text{overall Profit.}$$

(b) Twice overall Profit + Loss = Profit on the second.
∴ 20 + 10 = 30%

He should sell the 2nd box at 30% Profit.

9. **When prices rise by 20%, if the expenditure is to be the same, by what percentage the consumption is to be reduced?**

   Ans : New price is 120 and so we have to reduce 20 to keep the expenditure the same = $\frac{20}{120} \times 100$

   $= 16\frac{2}{3}\%$ consumption must be reduced.

10. **When prices fall by 10%, expenditure being the same, by what percentage the consumption has increased?**

    Ans: New Price is 90 and so we have to increase 10 to have the same expenditure. Increase in consumption

    $= \frac{10}{90} \times 100 = 11\frac{1}{9}\%$

    * M.P. - Marked Price   C.P.-Cost Price

    * M.P. - Market Price   S.P.-Selling Price

11. **A gets 20% more salary than B. So, B gets what percentage less salary than A?**

    Ans : 20% is $\frac{1}{5}$. So, if B gets 5, A gets 6.

    That is, B gets $\frac{1}{6}$ less of A's salary

    $\frac{1}{6} \times 100 = 16\frac{2}{3}\%$ Less.(Compare problem 9)

12. **If P gets 10% less salary than R, then R gets what percentage more salary than P?**

    Ans: 10% is $\frac{1}{10}$. So, if R gets 10, then P gets 9.

    That is R gets 1 more than P (or)

    $\frac{1}{9} \times 100 = 11\frac{1}{9}\%$ more. (Compare problem 10)

13. A reduction of Rs.6 in S.P. of an article will change 5% profit into $2\frac{1}{2}\%$ loss. What is the C.P. of the article?

   Ans: Difference between 5% Profit and $2\frac{1}{2}\%$ Loss is $7\frac{1}{2}\%$

   $7\frac{1}{2}\%$ = Rs.6

   So, C.P = $\dfrac{100 \times 2 \times 6}{15}$ = Rs. 80

14. A milk vendor buys 10 litres of milk at Rs.4 per litre and adds 6 litres of water. If he wants a profit of 50% at what rate he should sell this milk?

   Ans : $\dfrac{\text{Original Qty} + 50\% \text{ of Original Qty.}}{\text{Total Qty}} \times$ C.P. per litre

   $= \dfrac{10 + 50\% \text{ of } 10 \times 4}{10 + 6} = \dfrac{15 \times 4}{16} = $ Rs.3.75

15. A trader sells a cycle at 15% profit. If he had sold it for Rs.60 less, his loss would have been $1\frac{2}{3}\%$. What is the cost of the cycle?

   Ans : Difference between 15% (P) and $1\frac{2}{3}\%$ (L) is

   (ADD) = $16\frac{2}{3}\% = \dfrac{50}{300}$

   Cost = $\dfrac{60 \times 300}{50}$ = Rs. 360.

16. A salary amount if increased first by 15% and reduced later by 15%, what is the overall result?

   Ans : It is like marking the goods price 15% above C.P., and then giving a discount of 15% on M.P., while selling.

   In such cases, the answer is always "LOSS"

   $\dfrac{15^2}{10^2} = 1.5^2 = 2.25\%$ LOSS

17. A merchant sells goods for Rs.900 and gains $12\frac{1}{2}\%$. If he wants a gain of 15% for how much more he has to sell the goods?

   Ans : $900 \times \dfrac{100 + 15}{100 + 12\frac{1}{2}} = \dfrac{900 \times 115 \times 2}{225} = $ Rs.920 which is the new S.P. He has to sell for Rs.20 more.

18. A trader marks his goods at certain percentage above C.P. and after giving a discount of 5%, gains 33%. By how much percentage above the C.P. did he mark the price?

Ans : $\% = \dfrac{100(\text{Profit} + \text{Discount})}{100 - \text{Discount}}$

$= \dfrac{100 \times 38}{95} = 40\%$ above C.P.

19. A trader marks his goods 25% above C.P. and after giving discount on M.P., still gains $6\dfrac{1}{4}\%$. What is the rate of discount?

Ans : $\% = \dfrac{100(\text{Upward mark} - \text{Profit})}{100 + \text{Upward mark}}$

$\dfrac{100\left(25 - 6\frac{1}{4}\right)}{125} = \dfrac{4}{5} \times 18\dfrac{3}{4}$

$= \dfrac{4}{5} \times \dfrac{75}{4} = 15\%$ Discount rate.

20. A retailer marks his goods 20% above C.P. and then gives a rebate of 5% on the M.P. What is his percentage of profit or loss?

Ans : (Up rate − Rebate rate) − (5% of 20 (or) 20% of 5)

$= (20 - 5) - 1 = 14\%$ Profit

If in the above, the rebate is 18%, then

$(20 - 18) - 18\%$ of $20 = 2 - 3.6 = 1.6\%$ Loss.

21. Discount is $16\dfrac{2}{3}\%$ on M.P. Profit is 5%. What percent above the C.P. is the M.P.?

Ans : $16\dfrac{2}{3}\% = \dfrac{1}{6}$ Multiply Denominator 6 with 5 (P) and add

$1 \times 100 = 6 \times 5 + 100 = 130$

Divide 130 by (6 − 1) (Denominator − Numerator.)

$= \dfrac{130}{5} = 26.$

The M.P. is 26% above C.P.   (See problem 18)

Solve the Problems in Short-Cut Methods

22. If there is no discount in the above sum, what would be his profit?

Ans : 26%

23. M.P. is 40% above C.P. Profit is 19%. What is discount % on M.P.?

Ans : 40% is $\dfrac{2}{5}$

$$\text{Discount} = \dfrac{\text{Denominator (Mark above C.P. – Pro.)}}{\text{Numerator + Denominator}}$$

$$= \dfrac{5(40-19)}{5+2} = \dfrac{5}{7} \times 21 = 15\% \text{ Discount on M.P.}$$

(Pl. see problem 19)

24. If it is 2% Loss in the above problem, then discount on M.P. is

Ans : $\dfrac{5}{7} \times (40+2) = \dfrac{5}{7} \times 42 = 30\%$ which is Discount on M.P.

25. Discount on M.P. is 25%. Loss is 10%. What percentage above C.P. is the M.P.?

Ans : $(100-10) \times \dfrac{100}{(100-25)} = \dfrac{90 \times 100}{75} = 30 \times 4 = 120.$

which is M.P. It is 20% above C.P. (OR)

$25\% = \dfrac{1\,(N)}{4\,(D)}$. $4 \times 10\,(L) = 40$ and $100 - 40 = 60$

and $\dfrac{60}{D-N} = \dfrac{60}{3} = 20\%$ above C.P. (or)

(Den/D - Denominator, Num/N - Numerator

P Profit L - Loss)

$$\dfrac{(\text{Dis.}25 - \text{Loss}\,10) \times 100}{100 - \text{Dis.}} = 15 \times \dfrac{100}{75} = \dfrac{15 \times 4}{3} = 20\% \text{ above C.P.}$$

26. A retailer gives a discount of 10% on M.P. and gains 20%. If his gain is Rs.60 on an article sold, what is the M.P. of the article?

Ans : $\dfrac{60}{20} \times \dfrac{100+20}{100-10} \times 100 = \dfrac{3 \times 120 \times 100}{90} = $ Rs. 400 M.P.

Ex : Mental process: As $\dfrac{1}{5}$ profit is Rs.60, the C.P. is Rs.300 and so, the S.P. is Rs.360 which is $\dfrac{9}{10}$ part of M.P.

So M.P. is $\dfrac{360 \times 10}{9}$ = Rs. 400

This also gives that the M.P. is $\dfrac{1}{3}$ above C.P. or $33\dfrac{1}{3}$% above C.P.

27. **M.P. is 20% above C.P. Discount is 20% on M.P. What is the percentage of profit or loss?**

    Ans : When these two percentages are equal it is always LOSS

    % of Loss = $\dfrac{20^2}{10^2}$ = 4% LOSS.

    Note that, if there is to be no Loss, then the discount should be $\dfrac{20 \times 100}{120} = 16\dfrac{2}{3}\%$

28. **Gopu's salary was reduced by 10%. In order to have his original salary back, his salary now must be increased by what percent?**

    Ans : 10 is to be added now to 90, to get back 100

    (i.e.,) $\dfrac{1}{9} \times 100 = 11\dfrac{1}{9}\%$

    (See problem 10)

    (a) What happens if his reduced salary is increased by 10%?

    Ans : Well, he loses - By $\dfrac{10^2}{10^2}$ = 1% Loss

29. **A contractor was paid 10% more than what was due to him. What percentage of the new amount paid is to be recovered from him?**

    Ans : 110 is paid to pay 100. So 10 is to be recovered.

    % = $\dfrac{10}{110} \times 100 = 9\dfrac{1}{11}\%$

    (Pl. see problem 9)

30. **A retailer gives a discount of 20% on M.P. and gives a further discount of 10% on cash sale. What is the total percentage of the discount?**

    Ans : (20 + 10) − 10% of 20 = 30 − 2 = 28%

    Formula is $\left[(x+y) - \dfrac{xy}{100}\right]\%$

    (Compare problem 1)

31. The S.P. of an article was Rs.198 and the profit was 10%. If it was sold for Rs.2 more what would be the percentage of gain?

Ans : $\dfrac{\text{(New S.P.) } 200 \times (100+10)}{\text{Old S.P } 198} - 100$

$= \dfrac{110}{198} \times 200 - 100 = \dfrac{5}{9} \times 200 - 100$

$= \dfrac{1000 - 900}{9} = \dfrac{100}{9} = 11\dfrac{1}{9}\%$ which is new profit

If sold for Rs.8 less then,

$= \dfrac{110}{198} \times 190 - 100 = \dfrac{5}{9} \times 190 - 100 = \dfrac{950 - 900}{9}$

$= \dfrac{50}{9} = 5\dfrac{5}{9}\%$ New profit.

32. A retailer sells a box and suffers 15% loss. If he had sold it for Rs.36 more, he would have earned a profit of 10%. What was the Cost Price?

Ans: $\dfrac{36 \times 100}{15 + 10} = \dfrac{36 \times \cancel{100}^{4}}{\cancel{25}} = \text{Rs.}144$

(or) The difference between 15% Loss and 10% Profit is 25% (Added since one is L and the other G)

So 25% of C.P. = Rs.36. C.P. = 36 × 4 = Rs.144.

33. A wholesaler sells a chair for 15% profit. If he sells the same for Rs.6 less his profit will be 10%. What is the cost price of the chair?

Ans : Difference between 15% P and 10% P is 5% (since Both P)

5% or $\dfrac{1}{20}$ of cost is Rs.6

∴ C.P. = Rs.120.

34. A milk vendor buys 15 litres of milk at Rs.4.80 per litre and after adding water *sells* the mixture at the *same price*. If his gain is $33\dfrac{1}{3}\%$, how much water did he add?

Ans : $33\dfrac{1}{3}\% = \dfrac{1}{3}$. Water added = $\dfrac{15}{3} = 5$ litres.

(Since both C.P. and S.P. are same, they are not taken here for working)

Solve the Problems in Short-Cut Methods

35. A milk vendor bought 15 litres of milk at Rs.4.80 per litre and after adding some water sold the mixture at 20 paise more per litre and in the process gained 25%. How much water was added?

    Ans : With 25% Profit, the S.P. should be

    Rs.4.80 + Rs.1.20 = Rs.6.

    But it was sold at Rs.5 per litre.

    Qty. sold at this price was $\dfrac{6 \times 15}{5} = 18$ litres

    So 3 litres of water was added.

36. A trader cheats to the extent of 10% while buying as well as selling, by using false weights. What is his total gain?

    Ans : It means he pays Rs.90 for Rs.100 and gets Rs.110 for Rs.100. His total profit is Rs.20. that is
    $$\dfrac{20}{90} \times 100 = \dfrac{200}{9} = 22\dfrac{2}{9}\%$$

37. Successive discounts of 10% and 15% are equivalent to what discount?

    Ans : $\left[(x+y) - \dfrac{xy}{100}\right]\% = 25 - 1.5 = 23.5\%$.

38. An article was sold for Rs.6 more than C.P. The amount thus got by selling 5 articles covers the cost of 8 articles. What is the C.P. of each article?

    Ans : $\dfrac{\text{Amt. got more on Articles sold}}{\text{Diff. in Articles}} = \dfrac{5 \times 6}{8-5} = \dfrac{30}{3} = $ Rs.10

    which is C.P.

39. A dealer declares a discount of 20% on the M.P. and gives a further discount of 5% on cash sales. If he still gains 14% what percentage above the C.P. was the M.P.fixed?

    (L - Loss; G - Gain)

    Ans : Successive discounts of 20% and 5% are equal to

    $(20 + 5) - 5\%$ of $20 = 24\% = \dfrac{6}{25}\dfrac{N}{D}$

    So $\dfrac{25(\text{Den.}) \times 14 + 100 \times 6}{(\text{Den.} - \text{Num.})(25 - 6)} = \dfrac{950}{19} = 50\%$ above C.P. (OR)

$$= \frac{100(\text{Pro.} + \text{Dis.})}{100 - \text{Dis.}} = \frac{100 \times 38}{100 - 24} = \frac{100 \times 38}{76} = 50\% \text{ above C.P.}$$

(Pl. see problems 18, 21 and 25)

40. There is a book for sale. The amount got by selling it at $7\frac{1}{2}\%$ profit will be Rs.1.25 more than the amount got by selling it at 5% loss. What is the cost price?

    Ans : Total Difference $= 12\frac{1}{2}\% = \frac{1}{8}$

    So, C.P. = Rs.1.25 × 8 = Rs.10.

41. A man buys a dozen notebooks every month. If prices fall by 40%, how many notebooks more he will be able to buy for the same amount?

    Ans : Now for Rs.60 – 12 notebooks can be bought

    For Rs.100 $= \frac{12 \times 100}{60} = 20$ notebooks can be bought

    That is 8 notebooks more.

42. A boy buys a dozen fruits every week at the same price. In one week prices fell by 20% and for Re. 1, he got 2 fruits more. What was the C.P. of dozen fruits earlier?

    Ans : Old C.P. $= \dfrac{\text{Diff. on fruits over dozen}}{\text{fruits got more for Re.1}}$

    New price: Old price = 80 : 100 = 4 : 5

    ∴ For old price of one dozen, now 15 fruits can be bought.

    (i.e.,) 3 fruits more

    Substituting above, C.P. $= \frac{3}{2}$ = Rs.1.50 per dozen.

43. The M.P. of a mixie was Rs.600, and after giving a discount of $12\frac{1}{2}\%$, the profit was $16\frac{2}{3}\%$ What is the C.P.?

    Ans : Dis. $\frac{1}{8}$, Pro. $\frac{1}{6}$ C.P. $= 600 \times \frac{7}{8} \times \frac{6}{7} = $ Rs.450

    [It also means – $600 \times \dfrac{100 - \text{Dis.}}{100 + \text{Pro.}}$]

44. 2 cabinets costing Rs.650 and Rs.850 were sold at a profit of 20% and 40% respectively. What is the percentage of overall gain?

Ans : Cost ratio = 13:17. Profit ratio = 1:2 (Remember you have reduced by 20 times). Product = 13+34 = 47

Overall profit = $\dfrac{47 \times 20}{13+17}$ (since earlier we have reduced the profit by 20 times)

$= \dfrac{940}{30} = 31\dfrac{1}{3}\%$

Note that the above working is the mental process. If there is 20% Loss on the first, then overall profit is

$\dfrac{(34-13) \times 20}{30} = \dfrac{21 \times 2}{3} = 14\%$

45. A retailer sells goods for Rs.900 and gains $12\dfrac{1}{2}\%$. If he wants a profit of 15% for mow much he should sell the goods?

Ans : $900 \times \dfrac{100+15}{100+12\frac{1}{2}} = 900 \times \dfrac{115}{112\frac{1}{2}} = $ Rs.920 which is S.P.

He should sell for Rs.20 more.

46. If by selling for Rs.72, there is a loss of 10% then for how much the article must be sold to have a profit of 15%?

Ans : $72 \times \dfrac{100+15}{100-10} = \dfrac{72 \times 115}{90} = $ Rs.92. (Rs.20 More)

47. An article was sold for Rs.195, at a profit of 30%. What would be the profit or loss, if it is sold for (a)Rs.165 (b)Rs.140.

Ans : (a) $\dfrac{165}{195} \times (100+30) = \dfrac{11}{13} \times 130 = 110$

So Gain = 110 − 100 = 10% Gain.

(b) $\dfrac{140}{195} \times (100+30) = \dfrac{28}{39} \times 130 = \dfrac{280}{3} = 93\dfrac{1}{3}$

So Loss = $100 - 93\dfrac{1}{3} = 6\dfrac{2}{3}\%$ Loss.

48. In a village the population increased by 3% during some period. If 1400 persons were to be less than what it is, there would have been a decrease of 4%. Find the original population.

Ans : Difference between 3% increase and 4% decrease is 7%.

So population originally = $\dfrac{1400 \times 100}{7} = 20000$ persons.

49. A shopkeeper sells a Table-lamp for Rs.156 at a profit of 30%. If the cost price increases by 25% due to Tax levy;
    (a) for how much he should sell the article if there is no gain, or loss (which also means the C.P.)
    (b) If the article is sold for Rs.160, what is the new percentage of profit?
    (c) What would be the new percentage of profit, if there is no change in the original S.P.?

Ans : (a) $156 \times \dfrac{100+25}{100+30} = 156 \times \dfrac{125}{130} = $ Rs.150

which is also the C.P. after increase in Tax.

(b) $100 \times \left[\dfrac{160}{156} \times \dfrac{100+30}{100+25} - 1\right] = 100 \left[\left(\dfrac{40}{39} \times \dfrac{130}{125}\right) - 1\right]$

$= 100 \left(\dfrac{16}{15} - 1\right) = \dfrac{100}{15} = 6\dfrac{2}{3}\%$ new profit.

(c) $\dfrac{30-25}{100+25} \times 100 = \dfrac{5}{125} \times 100 = 4\%$ New profit.

(As there is no change in S.P. it is not taken for working out the result here).

50. A chemist who sold a bottle of Tonic noticed that if he had sold it for Rs.2 more he would have had 25% profit and, if he had sold it for Rs.2 less the profit would have been 5%. What is the cost price?

Ans : Both are profits. Hence difference = 20% (25 − 5)

Amount of one is less and the other is more.

Hence difference = Rs.4 (2 + 2)

20% is Rs.4. Cost Price = 4 × 5 = Rs.20.

51. A trader bought 120Kg. of coffee powder, and sold some part at 30% profit and the balance at 50% profit. If his overall profit was 45%, how much quantity was sold under each head?

Ans :   A   C   B
          30   45   50
          1st overall 2nd

Required Ratio = (50 − 45) : (45 − 30) = 5 : 15 = 1 : 3

∴ Qty. sold, at 30% Profit = $120 \times \dfrac{1}{4} = 30$ Kg.

∴ Qty. sold, at 50% Profit = $120 \times \dfrac{3}{4} = 90$ Kg.

52. An officer would pay the same Income tax, whether he paid a tax of 12% on his income above Rs.16,000 or, 10% on his income above Rs.14,200. What is his income?

Ans : Ratio of tax = 12:10 = 6:5

Ratio of the given income figure. (Divide by 1000) 16 : 14.2

Multiply ratio of tax with respective ratio of income = 96−71

(but at the end multiply the result by 1000)

Product Difference = 96 − 71 = 25

So Income 25 × 1000 = Rs.25,000

53. A man buys equal Number of two varieties of bananas at 6 per rupee and 10 per rupee respectively. He sells both at 16 for two rupees. What is the percentage of gain or loss?

Ans : Selling rate 8 for one rupee.

LCM of $\dfrac{6,10}{\text{bought}}$ and $\dfrac{8}{\text{Sold}}$ is 120

Ratio is $\dfrac{120}{6} : \dfrac{120}{10} : \dfrac{120}{8} = \dfrac{20:12}{\text{cost}} : \dfrac{15}{\text{sale}}$

Now (20 + 12) = 32 (Cost) is more than 2 × 15 = 30 (Sale)

So, there is Loss.

% of Loss = $\dfrac{32-30}{32} \times 100 = \dfrac{100}{16} = 6\dfrac{1}{4}$ % Loss.

54. A dealer bought 2 radios for Rs.1000. He sold both, one at 4% profit and the other at 10% loss. If his overall loss was 0.9%, what was the cost of each radio?

Ans : For Cost ratios   4 P   0.9 L   10 L

Overall

P. Art. : L. Art. = (10 − 0.9) :   (4 + 0.9)

since both are L   Since one is P and
another L

= 9.1 : 4.9 = 13 : 7

∴ Cost of one Radio (4% P) = $\dfrac{1000 \times 13}{20}$ = Rs.650.

Cost of other radio = Rs.350

Another formula:

If overall Loss then:- (Loss − Aggregate) : (Gain + Agg.)

= (10−0.9) : (4+0.9)

= 9.1 : 4.9 = 13 : 7   Rest follows as above.

55. Jim bought 2 articles for Rs.1100. He sold one at 16% profit and the other at 6% loss. If, on the whole there was no gain or loss, what was the cost of the articles?

   Ans : Here we can equate directly as there is no loss or gain

   (AGG - Aggregate, G - Gain)

   Cost of article showing Loss (A) × 6 = Cost of article showing Gain (B) × 16

   ∴ $\dfrac{A}{B} = \dfrac{16}{6} = \dfrac{8}{3}$

   Cost of (A) = 1100 × $\dfrac{8}{11}$ = Rs.800

   Cost of 2nd article = Rs.300

56. Two articles which were together bought for Rs.1000 were sold, one at 4% profit and the other at 10% loss, but there was an overall profit of 0.5%. What are the cost prices of the articles?

   Ans : Formula:- (L+Agg.Gain):(G-Agg. Gain)=(10+0.5) : (4 - 0.5)

   P.Art.   L.Art. =   3:1

   Cost = (P.Art) = 1000 × $\dfrac{3}{4}$ = Rs.750

   (L.Art) = Other = Rs.250

   Also: For ratio of Costs: 4P.   0.5P.   10L

                                           Overall

   P.Art.: L.Art = (10 + 0.5)   :   (4 − 0.5)

   Since one is P and another L   Since both P.

   = 10.5:3.5 = 3:1   Rest follows as above.

57. 2 watches were bought for Rs.600. One was sold for 12% profit and the other for 9% Loss. If there was a gain of Rs.30 overall, what was the cost of each watch?

Ans : Profit Rs.30 means – 5% Profit

Now for ratios 12P.   5P.   9L
                    Overall
COST RATIOS: (5 + 9)   (12 – 5)
               Since one is P   Since both are P.
               and another L
               = 14 : 7   = 2 : 1

Respective Costs = Rs.400 and Rs.200

Note : If in the above problem the total sale amount is given as Rs.630, then derive the profit as Rs.30 and proceed as above.

58. The cost of 2 articles are Rs.240 and Rs.360. The first one was sold for 15% profit and after selling the second, there was an overall profit of 3%. What was the percentage of gain, or loss on the second?

Ans : Ratio of Costs = 240 : 360 = 2:3

As Overall gain, ratio = (L + Agg.gain) : (G - Agg.gain)
                              P.Art.   L.Art.
                        = (L + 3) : (15 – 3) = 2:3
                        = 12

∴ L + 3 = 8. The Loss on 2nd article was 5%.

59. A dealer sold a T.V. for 4% profit and a Moped for 9% loss and suffered Rs.65 loss. If he had sold the T.V. and Moped at 9% profit and 4% loss respectively, he would have gained Rs.260. What were the cost price of T.V. and Moped together?

Ans : Difference between 4% Gain and 9% Loss + and 9% Gain and 4% Loss = 10 Units.

Amt. difference = 260 + 65 (since one is loss and another gain) = Rs.325.

∴ $\frac{1}{2}$ Cost of both is got by $\frac{325 \times 100}{10 \text{ Units}}$ = Rs.3250

Total Cost = Rs.6500

Now, take the first part. Rs.65 Loss means 1% L.

for ratio of Costs   T.V   Overall   Moped
                        4P   1L   9L

∴ Cost of T.V.: Cost of Moped = (9 – 1) : (4 + 1)

Since both L   Since one is P
              and another L

= 8 : 5

∴ Cost of T.V. = Rs.4000

Cost of Moped = Rs.2500

60. **A fruit dealer sells 50% of his stock at 50% profit and 25% of stock at 20% profit and the balance quantity gets damaged. What is his overall percentage of gain or loss?**

Ans : With S.P. (100+50) sale amount of 50% of stock = Rs.75

With S.P. (100+20) sale amount of 25% of stock = Rs.30

Total Sales = Rs.105*

so his profit is 5%

* If the figure obtained thus is 100 - No loss or gain. If it is less than 100 - Then there is loss.

61. **A furniture dealer gains 5%, if he sells a chair for Rs.84. He sells 60 chairs at that rate, and 40 more chairs at Rs.70 each. What is his overall percentage of gain or loss?**

Ans : C.P. of chair = $\dfrac{84 \times 100}{105}$ = Rs.80

Gain on 60 chairs = 60 × 4 = Rs.240

Loss on 40 chairs = 40 × 10 = Rs.400

Loss % = $\dfrac{160}{8000} \times 100 = 2\%$

62. **A trader marked his goods 40% above the cost price. He sold $\dfrac{1}{3}$ of goods giving 25% discount for cash sale, and the balance goods on credit giving 10% discount. What is his overall profit?**

Ans : Profit on $\dfrac{1}{3}$ of goods $\left[\dfrac{(40-25)-25\% \text{ of } 40}{100} \right] \times \dfrac{1}{3}$

$= \dfrac{15-10}{100} \times \dfrac{1}{3} = \left(\dfrac{5}{300} \right)$

Profit on $\dfrac{2}{3}$ of goods $= \left[\dfrac{(40-10)-10\% \text{ of } 40}{100} \right] \times \dfrac{2}{3}$

$$= \frac{30-4}{100} \times \frac{2}{3} = \left(\frac{52}{300}\right)$$

Total profit $= \frac{57}{300}$ or 19%

ANOTHER METHOD:

Dis	25	10	
% of stock	1	2	since $\frac{1}{3}$ & $\frac{2}{3}$
product	25	20	

Overall Discount $\frac{25+20}{1+2} = \frac{45}{3} = 15\%$

∴ Overall profit: (40 − 15) − 15% of 40 = 25 − 6 = 19%

Note that : (40 − 25) − 25% of 40

= 5 and [(40−10) − 10% of 40] = 26

Goods sold in ratio 1:2 ∴ Profit is got by

$$\frac{(5 \times 1) + (26 \times 2)}{2+1} = \frac{57}{3} = 19\%$$

63. A trader marked his goods 20% above C.P. He sold $\frac{3}{4}$ of stock at 10% discount on credit sale and the balance stock at some percentage of discount on cash sales. If his overall profit was 5%, what was the discount rate on the cash sale?

Ans : 5% overall profit means overall discount of

$$\frac{20-5}{120} \times 100 = \frac{15}{120} \times 100 = 12\frac{1}{2}\%$$

Goods sold in ratio 3:1 with discount on 1st at 10%.

The discount on cash sales = $12\frac{1}{2} \times (3+1) - (3 \times 10)$

= 50 − 30 = 20%.

64. A retailer sold a T.V. for 6% profit and a recorder for 10% profit and gained on the whole 7%. If he had sold the T.V. for 10% profit and recorder for 6% profit, he would have realised Rs.80 more in the sale amount. What are the cost of the articles?

Ans : From 1st part, T.V.6P. Overall 7P. Rec.10P.

Cost ratio of T.V.: Rec. = (10 − 7) : (7 − 6) = 3:1

Difference of (3 − 1) 2 units is equal to Rs.80.

Total amount = $\frac{80}{2} \times 100$ = Rs.4000

∴ Cost of T.V. = Rs.3000 and Cost of Recorder = Rs.1000.

Note that the % of profits on the articles in the 1st part are reversed on the same articles in the second part. Hence, this method.

65. **A whole sale dealer sells an Almirah for 20% profit and a steel cot for 30% profit and realises Rs.2240. If he had sold them both at 25% profit, he would have got Rs.10 more. What is the cost of the articles?**

   Ans :   A   -   C

   1st sale S.P.ratio   120 - 130   (Rs.2240)

   or   12   : 13 (224)

   2nd sale S.P.ratio   125 : 125 (Rs.2240+10=Rs.2250)

   or   1   : $1 \left(\frac{2250}{125} = 18 \right)$

   or   12   : 12 (216)

   or   13   : 13 (234)

   Diff.of 1 Unit on C (13-12) is equal to (224 – 216) = Rs.8

   For 100 Units = 8 × 100 = Rs.800 cost of cot.

   Difference of 1 unit on A (13 - 12) is equal to (234 – 224) = Rs.10.

   For 100 Units = 10 × 100 = Rs.1000 - Cost of Almirah.

66. **A trader was selling a cycle for Rs.678 and gaining 20% profit. When cost price fell by Rs.65, he reduced the sale price also by Rs.65. What was his new profit?**

   Ans : S.P.Rs.678; P.20%; C.P. = $678 \times \frac{5}{6}$ = Rs.565 & Profit Rs.113

   Now C.P. = 565 – 65 = Rs.500. No change in profit.

   New % of profit = $\frac{113}{500} \times 100 = \frac{113}{5}$ = 22.6%

   Also if C.P. = 100, S.P. = 120 or C.P. : S.P. = 5:6 (A:B)

   New % of profit

   $$= \frac{\text{Old S.P.} (B-A) \times 100}{\text{Old S.P.} \times A - B \times \text{Diff. in price}} = \frac{678 \times 1 \times 100}{678 \times 5 - 6 \times 65}$$

Solve the Problems in Short-Cut Methods

$$\frac{678 \times 100}{3390 - 390} = \frac{67800}{3000} = 22.6\%$$

SIMPLE METHOD:

(OR) Profit $= \dfrac{S.P. \times P}{100 + P} = \dfrac{678 \times 20}{120} =$ Rs.113

New Profit % $= \dfrac{113 \times 100}{678 - (113 + 65)} = \dfrac{11300}{500} = 22.6\%$

If C.P & S.P. are both increased by Rs.65 then

New Profit $= \dfrac{113 \times 100}{678 - (113 + 65)} = 17.936\%$

67. The cost of a jewel increased by 65% by passing through 3 dealers. If the first two had profits of 20% and 25% what was the profit of the third dealer?

Ans : The increase at the end of 2nd dealer = (20 + 25) + 25% of 20 = 45 + 5 = 50 and then the Cost was (100 + 50) = 150
Third increase of (65 – 50) = 15 was on 150

Third Profit $= \dfrac{15}{150} \times 100 = 10\%$

68. A sells a T.V. to B at 15% profit, and B sells the same to C at 10% profit. By how much percentage does the final sale price exceed the original price?

Ans : Total increase = (15 + 10) + 10% of 15
$\qquad\qquad\qquad = 25 + 1.5 = 26.5\%$.

69. The manufacturer makes 50% profit and, the wholesaler and retailer make profits of 20% and 10% respectively. By what percent the price increased finally?

Ans : Successive profits of 50% and 20% leads to increase of
(50 + 20) + 20% of 50 $\quad = 70 + 10 = 80\%$.
Successive profit of 80% and 10% (Last one) leads to
(80 + 10) + 10% of 80 $\quad = 90 + 8 = 98\%$.

If C.P. is Rs.250 final S.P. $= \dfrac{198}{100} \times 250 = 198 \times 2\dfrac{1}{2}$
$\qquad\qquad\qquad\qquad\quad = 396 + 99 =$ Rs.495

If final S.P. is Rs.396, the C.P. $= 396 \times \dfrac{100}{198} =$ Rs.200

70. A sells an article to B at 20% profit and B sells it to C giving a discount of 20%. If A had sold it direct to C at the same price paid by C, would it be gain or loss for A, and by what percentage?

Ans : It is the same as marking goods 20% above M.P. and giving a discount of 20% on M.P. It is also the same as if 2 articles were sold at the same price, gaining 20% on one and with a loss of 20% on the other:

So, Loss is 4% (i.e. $20^2/100$)

71. Out of students who applied for examination, 10% absented themselves. 25% of those who wrote the examination failed. If 135 students passed, how many applied for examination?

Ans : (It is similar to the problem where M.P. is asked, given that 10% rebate on M.P., and a further discount of 25% given for cash transaction)

We also know successive discounts of 10% and 25% is equal to 25% and 10% discounts given successively.

$\therefore$ (25 + 10) − 10% of 25 = 35 − 2.5 = 32.5%.

Failed = 32.5, passed = 67.5

Total Students = $\dfrac{135 \times 100}{67.5} = 200$

72. Some students wrote an examination, out of which 70% were boys and the rest girls. 45% of boys and 30% of girls failed. If the total students passed were 238, how many wrote the examination?

Ans : $\dfrac{B}{70} - \dfrac{G}{30}$ (or) 7:3 (10 times reduced)

Failed = (45) − (30).

i.e., Passed = 55, 70 (or) 5.5:7 (10 times reduced)

Total students = $\dfrac{238 \times 100}{7 \times 5.5 + 3 \times 7}$ (10×10 times above)

$= \dfrac{238 \times 100}{38.5 + 21} = \dfrac{238 \times 100}{59.5}$ = 400 Students.

73. A man bought some chairs and some tables for a total sum of Rs.6200. If he had bought as many tables as he bought chairs, and as many chairs as he bought tables, he would have paid Rs.1200 less. If the cost of a chair was Rs.60 and table Rs.100, how many chairs and tables he bought first?

Ans : Ist combination at Rs.60 – 100 (Rs.6200) or 3 - 5 (310)

IInd combination at Rs.100 – 60 (Rs.5000) or 5-3 (250)

Total C + T = $\dfrac{310+250}{3+5} = \dfrac{560}{8} = 70$ items.

Difference in items = $\dfrac{310-250}{5-3} = \dfrac{60}{2} = 30$

= (T – C)

∴ Tables = 50 & Chairs = 20.

73a. **What is the Number if 60% of it added to 60 gives the Number itself?**

Ans : To put it in other words a Number MINUS 60% of it is 60.

ie. 40% of Number is 60.

∴ The Number is 150.

74. In a shop selling gift items, a clock and light were sold at 9% profit and 10% loss respectively, and the overall loss was Rs.7. If they had been sold at 16% loss and 14% profit respectively, the gain would have been Rs.3. What are the costs of articles?

Ans :

	CL	LT
Write like this	9 -	10 (7)
	16 -	14 (3)
Make LT side common	63 -	70 (49)
	80 -	70 (15)

Cost of clock = $\dfrac{49-15}{80-63} \times 100 = 2 \times 100 = $ Rs.200

Make CL side common 144 - 160 (112)

144 - 126 (27)

Cost of Light = $\dfrac{112-27}{160-126} = \dfrac{85 \times 100}{34} = $ Rs.250.

75. A dealer sells 2 used T.Vs. each for Rs.2600. He gains 10% on one, and suffers loss of 5% on the other. What is his overall profit or loss percentage?

Ans : Write like this   P10   S.P.   110(A)

   L5   S.P.   95(B)

Cross multiply and find the difference. And divide it by (A + B)

Now 10×95 is more. So, there is profit. For % of profit

$$\frac{10 \times 95 - 5 \times 110}{110 + 95} = \frac{950 - 550}{205} = \frac{400}{205}$$

$$= \frac{80}{41} = 1\frac{39}{41}\%$$

Note : The actual cost price or S.P. has no bearing in the working.

Note : If it is asked what should be the percentage of gain on the first to compensate the loss of 5% on the second,

then :- L5 SP 95

The profit on Ist should be $\dfrac{5 \times 100}{95 - 5} = \dfrac{500}{90} = 5\dfrac{5}{9}\%$

76. A dealer of furniture marks his goods 40% above the cost price. If he sells the items at cost price what is the discount on marked price given?

Ans: 40% is 2/5. Add two zeros to the Numerator and for the denominator add 2 + 5 = 7

The answer is $\dfrac{200}{7} = 28\dfrac{4}{7}\%$. Note the mental process.

❈ ❈ ❈

TIME AND DISTANCE

1. **A boat crosses a distance of 30km in 5hrs downstream, and takes 6hrs to cover the same distance upstream. What is the speed of the boat? (or of current?)**

   Ans : We may take the speed of boat and speed of current as $(6+5) : (6-5) = 11:1$ which gives speed downstream as $11+1 = 12$kmph and in 5hrs covers $5 \times 12 = 60$km. But the distance given is only 30km. So the speed of boat is $\frac{11}{2} = 5\frac{1}{2}$ kmph. Hence speed of current is $\frac{1}{2}$ kmph. Note the mental process of working.

2. **A young man goes in a boat 20km upstream and returns to the starting point. If the speed of current is 4kmph and the boat speed in still water is 12kmph, what is the average speed?**

   Ans : In such problems the distance is immaterial, as it is the same up and down.

   Speed downstream & upstream are $(12 + 4) \times (12 - 4)$
   (i.e.) 16kmph $\times$ 8kmph

   Average speed $= \dfrac{\frac{16 \times 8}{16+8}}{2} = \dfrac{128}{12} = 10\frac{2}{3}$ kmph

3. **The ratio of speed of a boat downstream to upstream is 7:2. What is the ratio of its speed in still water and speed of current?**

   Ans : $(7 + 2) : (7 - 2) = 9:5$

4. **A boat takes 55 min. downstream from P to Q and 75 min. upstream from Q to P. What is the ratio of speed in still water and speed of current?**

   Ans : $(55 + 75) : (75 - 55) = 130 : 20 = 13 : 2$

5. **The speed of a boat in still water is 7kmph and the speed of current is 3kmph. A boat goes from P to Q and Q to P back in $10\frac{1}{2}$ hrs. What is the distance between P and Q?**

   Ans : Speed Down Stream $\times$ SP.UP ST

   $= (7 + 3) (7 - 3) = 10 \times 4 = 40$

$$\text{Average speed} = \frac{40}{4+3} = \frac{40}{7} \text{ kmph}$$

Distance from P to Q + Q to P

$$= \frac{40}{7} \times 10\frac{1}{2} = \frac{40}{7} \times \frac{21}{2} = 60 \text{ km}$$

Distance from P to Q $= 30$ km.

6. The speed of current is $4\frac{1}{2}$ kmph. The time taken to go upstream is 4 times the time taken to go the same distance downstream. What is the speed in still water?

   Ans: Ratio of time Downstream : Upstream $= 1 : 4$

   Speed in still water : Speed of Current $= (4 + 1) : (4 - 1)$

   $\qquad\qquad\qquad\qquad\qquad\qquad\quad = 5 : 3$

   Speed in still water $= 4\frac{1}{2} \times \frac{5}{3} = \frac{9}{2} \times \frac{5}{3} = 7\frac{1}{2}$ kmph

7. A launch goes downstream and upstream, the same distance and the average speed is $3\frac{1}{3}$ kmph. If the speed upstream is 2 kmph, what is the speed downstream and speed in still water?

   Ans: Average speed $=$

   $$\frac{\text{SP.D.S} \times \text{SP.U.S}}{\frac{1}{2}(\text{SP.D.S} + \text{SP.U.S})} = \frac{2(\text{SP.D.S} \times \text{SP.U.S})}{(\text{SP.D.S} + \text{SP.U.S})}$$

   $\therefore \dfrac{10}{3 \times 2} = \dfrac{\text{SPD.S} \times 2}{\text{SPD.S} + 2}$; $12\,\text{SP.D.S} = 10\,\text{SP.D.S} + 20$

   $\qquad\qquad\qquad = 2\,\text{SP.D.S} = 20$ (or) SP.D.S $= 10$ kmph

   (D.S./Down st - Downstream U.S./UPST - Upstream
   AVR/AVE - Average SP-Speed)

   SP. in still water $= \dfrac{\text{SP.D.S} + \text{SP.U.S}}{2} = \dfrac{10+2}{2} = 6$ kmph

   Sp. of current $= 10 - 6 = 4$ kmph

8. The speed of a launch in still water is $7\frac{1}{2}$ kmph. It goes 24 km downstream in the same time it goes 6 km upstream. What is the speed of the current?

   Ans: Time is same. So, speeds are in proportion to the distance covered.

∴ SP.D.S. : SP.U.S. = 24 : 6 = 4:1

That is SP, in still water and SP.of current are in ratio $(4 + 1) : (4 - 1) = 5 : 3$.

So, speed of current $= \dfrac{7\frac{1}{2} \times 3}{5} = 4\frac{1}{2}$ kmph

9. **A cyclist goes some distance at 16kmph and returns the same distance at 10kmph. What is his average speed?**

   Ans : In such problems the distance makes no difference.

   Average speed $= \dfrac{16 \times 10}{\frac{16+10}{2}} = \dfrac{160 \times 2}{26} = \dfrac{160}{13} = 12\dfrac{4}{13}$ kmph

10. **In the problem above if the onward speed is 16kmph and return speed is 12kmph and the whole journey takes $1\frac{3}{4}$ hrs, what is the total distance covered?**

    Ans : AVR.speed $= \dfrac{16 \times 12}{\frac{16+12}{2}} = \dfrac{16 \times 12}{14}$ kmph

    Total distance covered $= \dfrac{16 \times 12}{14} \times \dfrac{7}{4} = 24$ km

    Which also gives one way journey = 12km.

11. **A boy walked to school at $2\frac{1}{4}$ kmph. If he had walked $\frac{1}{4}$ km an hour faster, he would have reached school 8 Minutes earlier. What is the distance to the school?**

    Ans: $\dfrac{\text{Time Difference in min.}}{60 \text{ (To convert into HRS)}} \times \dfrac{\text{Product of 2 speeds}}{\text{Difference in speed}}$

    $= \dfrac{8}{60} \times \dfrac{2\frac{1}{4} \times 2\frac{1}{2}}{\frac{1}{4}} = \dfrac{8}{60} \times \dfrac{9}{4} \times \dfrac{5}{2} \times \dfrac{4}{1} = 3$ km

12. **In the problem above if it is given that - had he walked $\frac{1}{4}$ km an hour slower, he would have reached school 8 minutes late, then the distance is....**

    Ans : $= \dfrac{8}{60} \times \dfrac{2 \times 2\frac{1}{4}}{\frac{1}{4}} = \dfrac{8}{60} \times \dfrac{18}{4} \times \dfrac{4}{1} = \dfrac{12}{5} = 2.4$ km

SURA'S ❖ Solve the Problems in Short-Cut Methods

13. A man walks from his office at 3kmph and reaches home 15 min. late. If he has walked at 4kmph, he would have reached 10 min. early. What is the distance covered?

    Ans : Same as in (ii)
    $$\frac{15+10}{60} \times \frac{4 \times 3}{4-3} = \frac{25}{60} \times \frac{12}{1} = 5 \text{km}$$

14. A man going at a speed of 4.8kmph reaches his destination 15 min. *early*. If he goes the same distance at a speed of 6kmph, he reaches the destination 30 min. *early*. What is the distance covered?

    Ans : Both times given are 'early'. Hence DEDUCT
    Time Diff. $\frac{(30-15)}{60} \times \frac{6 \times 4.8}{6-4.8} = \frac{1}{4} \times \frac{6 \times 4.8}{1.2} = 6 \text{km}$
    (To convert into Hrs)

    Note : Similar is the working if both time differences given are 'late'.

15. Tom and Sam start from A with speeds of 12kmph and 15kmph respectively, and reach B. Sam starts 1 hour *after* Tom and reaches B, 1 hour 6 min. *before* Tom. What is the distance between A and B points?

    Ans :
    Note : Time differences are one 'after' and other 'before'. So we add.
    $$\frac{\text{Product of speeds}}{\text{Difference in speeds}} \times \text{Time difference}$$
    $$= \frac{12 \times 15}{15-12} \times \left(1 + 1\frac{1}{10}\right) = \frac{180}{3} \times \frac{21}{10} = 126 \text{km}$$

    Note : In the above problem, Tom may start 1 hour before Sam and reach destination 1 hour 6 min after Sam. Working is the same.

16. A and B go from P to Q at speeds 10kmph and 12kmph respectively. A starts 35 min. *after* B and reaches Q, 100 min. *after* B. What is the distance between P and Q?

    Ans: Note : Time differences are both 'after'. Hence DEDUCT.
    $$\frac{10 \times 12}{12-10} \times \frac{65}{60} = \frac{120}{2} \times \frac{65}{60} = 65 \text{km}$$
    (To convert into Hour)

Note : In the above problem B may start 35 min. *before* A and reach Q 100 min. *before* A. Working is the same.

17. A motorist travels from A to B, a distance of 512km. He goes $\frac{3}{8}$ of distance at 25kmph and the rest at 50kmph. What is his average speed?

   Ans : Write down as given $\frac{(P) \ 3}{(Q) \ 8}$ at 25kmph (R)

   Balance of distance $\frac{(S) \ 5}{(Q) \ 8}$ at 50kmph (T)

   $$\frac{\text{LCM of R,T} \times Q}{\left(\frac{T}{R}\right) \times P + S} = \frac{50 \times 8}{(2 \times 3) + 5} = \frac{400}{11}$$

   $= 36\frac{4}{11}$ kmph.

   Note : For average speed, the actual distance travelled has no relevance here.

18. A salesman travels 90km by auto, 330km by train, and 30km by boat and completes the whole journey in 12hrs 20 min. If the speed of train is 3 times that of the boat and $1\frac{1}{2}$ times that of the auto, what is the speed of the train?

   Ans : SPEEDS Ratio T:A:B = 3:2:1

   Time taken will be $\frac{330}{3} + \frac{90}{2} + \frac{30}{1}$ = 110 + 45 + 30

   = 185 hrs.

   Correct speeds will be $\frac{185}{12\frac{1}{3}}$ Times of 3:2:1

   $\frac{185 \times 3}{37} \times (3:2:1) = 15 \times (3:2:1)$

   The speeds of T,A, & B are 45kmph, 30kmph & 15kmph.

20. A scooterist travelled 135km, part at 15kmph and the balance distance at 18kmph. If he takes 8 hours to cover the distance of 135km, how much distance was covered under different speeds?

   Ans : Follow carefully. If the entire journey of 8 hours was at 15 kmph, the distance covered will be 120km. The extra, or difference of (135−120) = 15km is due to the speed difference of (18−15) = 3kmph, by the distance covered at 18 kmph.

∴ Distance covered at 18kmph = $\frac{15}{3} \times 18$ = 90km. So, the other distance covered at 15kmph was 45km.

In figures: $\frac{135-(8\times 15)}{18-15} \times 18 = 90$km at 18kmph

$\frac{(18\times 8)-135}{18-15} \times 15 = 45$km at 15kmph

The following method is also very important.

Time required if all distance is covered at 15kmph = 9hrs.

Time required if all distance is covered at 18kmph = $\frac{15}{2}$ hrs.

Actual Time = 8hrs.

Write ratio as given and equalise 9   8 $\frac{15}{2}$

                                                 Actual

or   18   16   15

So, the distances are in Ratio (16 − 15) : (18 − 16)

                                                = 1 : 2

That is distance covered at 15kmph = 45km
and distance covered at 18kmph = 90km

21. **In a race a scooterist had a start of 48 min. If he went at 20kmph and another scooterist followed him at 28kmph, when will the latter meet the former?**

   Ans : Note that a start of 48 min. is equal to a distance of $\frac{48}{60} \times 20 = 16$km. They are going in the same direction.

                                               (So deduct speeds)

So, their meeting time = $\frac{16}{28-20} = \frac{16}{8} = 2$hrs. after the latter starts

Note that this also gives us the distance from the starting point, at which they meet 2 × 28 = 56km.

22. In a 200 M Race, B starts 35 M before A, but A wins the race while B is still 15 M behind. What is the ratio of their speeds, assuming both start at the same time?

   Ans : While A runs 200 M, B runs 200 − (35 + 15) = 150 M

   ∴ Their speeds are in ratio 4:3.

23. A motorist going at 9kmph less than normal speed covers a distance in 3 hours more than the normal time.

   If he had gone at 16kmph more than normal speed he would have covered the same distance in 2 hours less time than normal.

   What was the distance and normal speed?

   Ans : (Problems like this are usually done using x,y etc) write like this:-

   (A) 9kmph less   − 3 hrs. more (B)
   (C) 16kmph more − 2 hrs. less (D)

   Normal Time =

   $$\frac{9 \times 3 \times 2 + 16 \times 2 \times 3}{9 \times 2 \sim 16 \times 3} \quad \frac{A \times B \times D + C \times D \times B}{A \times D \sim B \times C}$$

   ~ denotes deduct lower number from higher number

   $$= \frac{54 + 96}{30} = \frac{150}{30} = 5 \text{ Hours (or)} \left[\frac{B \times D (A + C)}{A \times D \sim B \times C} \right]$$

   $$\frac{16 \times 9 \times 3 + 9 \times 16 \times 2}{9 \times 2 \sim 16 \times 3} \quad \frac{A \times C \times D + B \times A \times C}{A \times D \sim B \times C}$$

   $$\text{Speed} = \frac{432 + 288}{30} = \frac{720}{30} = 24 \text{ kmph} \left[\frac{A \times C (B + D)}{A \times D \sim B \times C} \right]$$

   ∴ Distance = 24 × 5 = 120 km.

24. (When the increase, or decrease is in some fixed portion of the S.P., the problem may be easily solved through mental process, without actually finding out the C.P.) A cycle was sold for Rs.392 at a profit of 40%. When the cost price fell by Rs.28, the sale price was also reduced by the same margin. What is the new profit percentage?

   Ans : We know 40% profit means CP:SP = 100:140 = 5:7

   The reduction of Rs.28 is $\frac{1}{14}$ of the S.P.

Multiply this by $\frac{7}{5} = \frac{1}{10}$.

The new % profit = $40 \times \frac{10}{10-1} = \frac{400}{9} = 44\frac{4}{9}\%$

Note : 1. Rs.28 represents $\frac{1}{10}$ of cost price.

2. If the C.P. has increased by Rs.28 and the S.P. too increased by the same margin, then the profit will be

$$40 \times \frac{10}{10+1} = \frac{400}{11} = 36\frac{4}{11}\%$$

25. Do lengthy problems need lengthy working to find the solution? Well, not always. Take this problem:

A trader bought 2 articles for Rs.1500. If he sells the first article for 16% profit and the second article at 8% profit, he will get Rs.12 more than if he sells the first article for 12% profit and the second for 10% profit. What are the cost of the two articles?

In the usual method you may assume the cost of the 1st as Rs x and the cost of the second as Rs $(1500 - x)$ and solve for x (or, Rs x × Rs y, say) But, can we do it mentally?

Ans : Entry in the mental frame   A —— B —— (A + B) $\frac{\text{Diff.}}{12}$

16 —— 8 —— 1500

12 —— 10

If both the articles were sold A at 4% higher (16 − 12) then the extra amount would have been Rs.60. But, the difference given is only Rs.12. So, the further difference of Rs.48 is due to the differences in (16 − 12) and (10 − 8) = 4 and 2. Since there is increase on one and decrease on the second ADD 4 + 2 = 6.

So, 6% Diff = Rs.48   Cost of B = Rs.800

∴ Cost of A = Rs.700

Suppose we start with B.

If both articles were sold for 2% less (10 − 8), then the difference would have been Rs.30 LESS. But, the given difference is Rs.12 more. So total difference = Rs.42 (ADD because one is more, the other is less)

So, 6% difference = Rs.42   Cost of A = Rs.700

∴ Cost of B = Rs.800

26. There are two cans, each of 5 litre capacity. In one (A) there is 4 litres of milk and in the other (B) there is 4 litres of water.

First, the contents of B is poured into (A) to fill it, and then the contents of (A) is poured to fill (B) and in the third operation the contents of (B) is poured into (A) again to fill it.

What is the ratio of milk and water in (A) after the third operation?

Ans : Note that capacity of the cans and the contents in them are equal.

      (A) 5 LIT   (B) 5 LIT
        4(M)   4(W)

After 1st operation we have in can (A) 4 M:1W and in (B) 3 lit. water.

Note ratio is 4:1. Total is 5. Difference is 3. C:D

After 2nd operation the W:M in can (B) will be $C+D = 5^2$ and difference 3^2.

∴ Ratio of W:M = 17:8

After 3rd operation the M:W in can (A) will be $C+D = 5^3$ and difference 3^3.

∴ Ratio of M:W in (A) = 76:49

$$\% = \frac{76}{125} \times 100 = \frac{76 \times 4}{5} = \frac{304}{5} = 60.8\%$$

27. **COROLLARY:** What would be the ratio after 3rd operation, in vessel B, if we had poured first from (A) to (B)?

Ans: It would be the reverse of the one above (i.e.) 49:76.

28. A 10 litre can is full of pure milk. 4 litres of this is removed and the same quantity of water is added. Again 4 litres of this adulterated milk is removed and 4 litres of water is added. Once again 4 litres of this mixture is removed and same quantity of water is added. What is the strength of milk in the can now? (or, what is the ratio of milk and water?)

Ans : Note that the quantity of milk removed once and the water substituted is the same in the three operations. Remember 10 and that 10 – 4 = 6.

The ratio of Milk: Water after 1st operation

$$\begin{array}{r}M : W\end{array}$$

is 6 : (10 − 6) = 6 : 4 = 3 : 2

After second operation $6^2 : (10^2 − 6^2) = 36 : 64 = 9:16$

After third operation $6^3 : (10^3 − 6^3) = 216 : 784$
$$= 27:98$$

Strength of milk $= \dfrac{27}{125} \times 100 = \dfrac{108}{5} = 21.6\%$

M : W

ALSO Note that after 1st operation the ratio is 3 : 2 (Total 5)

At the end of 2nd operation ratio $= 3^2 : (5^2 − 3^2) = 9:16$

At the end of 3rd operation ratio $= 3^3 : (5^3 − 3^3) = 27 : 98$

29. **COROLLARY:-** Can we solve it the easy way, even if the quantities differ in each operation? Yes. Why not?

Suppose first-removed 4 lit. and equal qty of water is added, and secondly 3 lit. is removed and same qty of water is added and thirdly 2 lit. is removed and same qty. of water is added.

Ans: At the end of 3rd operation ratio of M:W, will be

$[(10 − 4) \times (10 − 3) \times (10 − 2)] : 10^3$ − L.H.S.

$= (6 \times 7 \times 8) : [10^3 − (6 \times 7 \times 8)]$

$= 336 : 664 = 42:83$

The % of milk will be $\dfrac{42}{125} \times 100 = \dfrac{168}{5} = 33.6\%$

30. A cloth merchant sold a Benares Saree and a Kashmir Saree at a profit of 3% and 5% respectively. If he had sold them at 5% & 7% profit respectively he would have got Rs.20/- more. The cost of the sarees are (a) Rs.340, Rs.650 (b) Rs.660, Rs.420 (c) Rs.560, Rs.440 (d) Rs.290, Rs.720. (Tick the correct answer).

Ans : There is no need to assume the cost of sarees as Rs.'x' and Rs.'y' and proceed to solve two equations.

See that the increase (or decrease) in percentage is the same for both articles (i.e.) 2%.

Cost of both, therefore, if 2% = Rs. 20 will be Rs.1000

Note that only (c) gives the total of Rs.1000, which is the correct answer.

You may also note that in such cases where the increase or decrease in % is the same for both articles; it will be difficult to find the cost of each article. Because, 2% of A + 2% of B = Rs. 20

or A+B = Rs.1000. That is, this difference of Rs.20 will be the same, irrespective of the cost of each article, provided of course the total of both is Rs.1000. Ex.:- Rs.100, Rs.900; Rs.350, Rs.650.

Let us solve a few more problems without lengthy working.

31. **2 articles were bought and sold at 2% and 3% profit respectively. If they were sold at 3% and 5% profit respectively, the trader would have got Rs.14.40 more. If instead of 3% & 5%, they were sold at 3% (P) and 2% (P) respectively he would have got only Rs.1.20 more. What is the cost price of the articles?**

   Ans : We have here 2 equations on the differences.

   1% (A) + 2% (B) = Rs.14.40 (or) A + 2B = 1440

   1% (A) − 1% (B) = Rs.1.20 (or)   A − B = 120

   Solving we have B = Rs.440 and   A = Rs.560

   L.H.S.-Left hand side   R.H.S.-Right hand side   MPS-Miles per second

32. **A dealer buys 2 articles for a total of Rs.1000/- If he sells the first one at 2% profit and the second at 3% profit he gets Rs.4 more than the amount he gets when he sells the first one at 3% and the second at 2% profit. What is the cost price of articles?**

   Ans : There is a decrease of 1% on the second and an increase of 1% on the 1st, but the first combination gets more. So, cost of 'B' is more.

   We have equation 1% of B − 1% of A = 4

   or B − A   = 400

   and A + B   = 1000

   Solving we get B = Rs. 700 & A = Rs. 300

33. **Given that cost of A + Cost of B = Rs.1000. Selling at 2% (P) on A and 3% (P) on B, gets Rs.50 more than the selling at 3% (L) on A and 2% (L) on B. What is the cost of each article?**

[72]

Ans : We have
	A	B	
	2% P	3% P	— Rs. 50 more
	3% L	2% L	—

The equations are $(2 + 3)\%$ of $A + (3 + 2)\%$ of $B = 50$

or $5A + 5B = 5000$

which gives $A + B = Rs. 1000$ Hence not possible to find out the individual prices.

34. Suppose it is given $A + B = Rs. 1000$,

	A	B	
and sale at	2% P	3% P	gets Rs.64 more than
sale at	3% L	4% L.	

Then we have equation $A + B = 1000$

and $[5\%$ of $A + 7\%$ of $B = 64]$

(or) $5A + 7B = 6400$

and $5A + 5B = 5000$

solving we get $B = Rs. 700$ & $A = Rs. 300$

35. Suppose it is given that $A + B = Rs. 1000$ and,

	A	B	
	5% P	2% L	sale amount gets Rs.44 more than
sale on	3% L	8% P.	The first combination gets more.

So it is obvious cost of A is more than cost of B.

So $(5 + 3)\%$ of $A - (2 + 8)\%$ of $B = 44$.

or $8A - 10B = 4400$ (or) $4A - 5B = 2200$

and $\underline{8A + 8B = 8000}$ $\underline{4A + 4B = 4000}$

$18B = 3600$ $9B = 1800$

or $B = Rs. 200$ and $A = Rs. 800$

36. **A 125 metre long train overtakes a man walking parallel in the same direction with a speed of 4 kmph, in 9 seconds. What is the speed of the train?**

Ans : 125 Mtrs in 9 Sec. $= \dfrac{125}{9} \times \dfrac{18}{5} = 50$ kmph

Since the direction is same Add 4

Speed of train = 54kmph.

Note: If the man was walking in opposite direction the speed of train = 50 − 4 = 46kmph.

37. A train going at 45kmph, crosses a man going on a cycle in the same direction in 15 seconds. If he were to be going in the opposite direction, it would have taken only 10 seconds to cross him. What is the length of the train?

Ans : $45\text{kmph} = \dfrac{45 \times 5}{18} = \dfrac{25}{2}$ MPS

Ratio of time in opp direction: Same direction
= 10:15 = 2:3

Ratio of speed in opp direction: Same direction = 3:2

Speed of Train : Speed of man = (3 + 2) : (3 − 2) = 5:1

Length of train = $\dfrac{25}{2} \times \left(\dfrac{5+1}{5}\right) \times \dfrac{10}{1} = 150$M

or

$\dfrac{25}{2} \times \dfrac{(5-1)}{5} \times 15 = 150$M

38. The speed of three goods trains are 50kmph, 35kmph & 25kmph. If these trains go from station A to B, a distance of 360km, what is the ratio of the time taken by them?

Ans : Speed's Ratio = 50 : 35 : 25 = 10:7:5

L.C.M. = 70

Ratio of Time = $\dfrac{70}{10} : \dfrac{70}{7} : \dfrac{70}{5} = 7 : 10 : 14$

Note: Since the ratio is asked, the actual distance has no relevance.

39. A student going at 4kmph notices that a 90 Metre long train going in the opposite direction crosses him in 6 seconds. What is the speed of the train?

Ans : $\dfrac{18}{5}$ (To convert into km) $\times \dfrac{90}{6} = 3 \times 18 = 54$kmph.

Speed of Train = 54 − 4 = 50kmph.

Note : If the boy was going in the same direction the speed of train will be 54 + 4 = 58kmph.

40. A passenger standing on a Railway platform notices that a goods train going West crosses him in $7\frac{1}{2}$ seconds and another goods train of same length and going East crosses him in 10 seconds. In how much time the two trains cross each other?

   Ans : The trains are going in opposite direction. The required time is got by

   $$= \frac{2 \times 10 \times 7\frac{1}{2}}{10 + 7\frac{1}{2}} = \frac{150}{17\frac{1}{2}} = \frac{150 \times 2}{35} = \frac{60}{7} = 8\frac{4}{7} \text{ Sec.}$$

41. An express train and a passenger train start at the same time from stations P and Q and proceed towards Q and P with speeds 64kmph and 36kmph respectively. By the time they meet, the express has travelled 140km more than the passenger train. What is the distance between the two stations?

   Ans : Apply formula:-
   $$\text{Sum of speeds} \times \frac{\text{Distance travelled more}}{\text{Difference in speeds}}$$
   $$= 100 \times \frac{140}{28} = 500 \text{ km}$$ which is the distance between stations.

   Note that it also implies that the passenger has travelled 140km less.

42. 2 trains of length 130M and 150M, going in opposite directions cross each other in 8 seconds and while going in the same direction cross each other in 56 seconds. What are their speeds?

   Ans : In Opp. Direction $\frac{130 + 150}{8} = 35$ M in 1 sec.

   In Same Direction $\frac{130 + 150}{56} = 5$ Metre in 1 sec.

   Speed of one train $= \frac{35 + 5}{2} \times \frac{18}{5}$ (convert mps to kmph)

   $$= \frac{40}{2} \times \frac{18}{5} = 72 \text{ kmph}$$

   Speed of 2nd train $= \frac{35 - 5}{2} \times \frac{18}{5} = 54 \text{ kmph}$

Note that the actual length of each train makes no difference so long the total length is 280 M.

43. A constable on beat notices that if he walks at 2kmph less speed he would cover the planned distance in 3 hours and, if he goes at 4kmph more speed, he would cover the same distance in only 45 min. What is his speed and distance?

Ans : $\dfrac{(\text{Less speed} \times \text{Hours}) + (\text{More speed} \times \text{Hours})}{\text{Diff.in corresponding hours}}$

$= \dfrac{(2 \times 3) + (4 \times 3/4)}{3 - 3/4} = \dfrac{6+3}{9/4} = \dfrac{9 \times 4}{9} = 4$ kmph Speed

Distance $= (4-2) \times 3 = 6$km or $(4+4) \times \dfrac{3}{4} = 6$km.

44. 2 trains, each 350m long are going in opposite directions with speeds of 30kmph and 40kmph respectively. How much is the time taken by the slower train to pass the driver of the faster train?

Ans : Do not get confused. The distance covered is the length of the slower train. It is just like crossing a cyclist coming in the opposite direction. The length of the 2nd train makes no difference.

Time in seconds $= \dfrac{350}{(40+30)} \times \dfrac{18}{5} = 18$ Sec.

45. A cyclist going at a speed of $2\dfrac{1}{2}$ metres per second notices that a 140M long train going in the same direction crosses him completely in 8 sec. What is the train's speed?

Ans : Distance in one sec. $= \dfrac{140}{8} = 17\dfrac{1}{2}$ Mps. Same direction. So, add person's speed to get the train speed.

$17\dfrac{1}{2} + 2\dfrac{1}{2} = 20$ Mps (or) $\dfrac{20 \times 18}{5} = 72$kmph.

46. A train crosses a man going on a cycle at $2\dfrac{1}{2}$ Mps in the same direction in 16 seconds and a platform of length 365 metres in 48.5 sec. What is its speed and length?

Ans : In (48.5 - 16) sec. the train covers a distance of 365 metres.
The distance covered in 16 sec. at $2\frac{1}{2}$ Mps = 40 M.
Same direction. So train covers actually 365 – 40 = 325 metres in 32.5 sec. (i.e.) 10 M in one second.

So speed = $\dfrac{10 \times 18}{5}$ = 36 kmph

At 10 Mps, Dist. travelled in 48.5 sec. = 485 m.
Platform = 365 m.
Train length = 125m

❈ ❈ ❈

TIME AND WORK

1. A can do a piece of work in 12 days, and B can do the same in 15 days. In how many days can both do it?

   Ans : $\dfrac{12 \times 15}{12 + 15} = \dfrac{180}{27} = \dfrac{60}{9} = 6\dfrac{2}{3}$ days.

2. Tom can do a piece of work in 16 days. Tom and John together can do it in 10 days. In how many days can John alone do the work?

   Ans : $\dfrac{16 \times 10}{16 - 10} = \dfrac{160}{6} = \dfrac{80}{3} = 26\dfrac{2}{3}$ days.

3. A, B and C can do a work separately in 12, 15 and 20 days. In how many days can the three together do it?

   Ans : $\dfrac{12 \times 15 \times 20}{(12 \times 15) + (15 \times 20) + (20 \times 12)} = \dfrac{12 \times 15 \times 20}{180 + 300 + 240}$

   $\dfrac{12 \times 15 \times 20}{720} = 5$ days.

4. A+B can do a work in 6 days and the same work can be done by B+C in 10 days or C+A in 12 days. In how many days the three together can complete the work?

   Ans: $\dfrac{6 \times 10 \times 12}{(6 \times 10) + (10 \times 12) + (12 \times 6)}$ multiply by $2 = \dfrac{720 \times 2}{60 + 120 + 72}$

   $= \dfrac{720 \times 2}{252} = 5\dfrac{5}{7}$

5. Ram and Shyam can complete a work separately in 10 days and 15 days respectively. If they work alternate days starting with Ram, when will the work be completed?

   Ans : It will be double the time taken by both working every day.

   $\therefore 2 \times \dfrac{10 \times 15}{15 + 10} = \dfrac{300}{25} = 12$ days.

6. Peter, Tom and John can do a work separately in 3 days, 6 days and 9 days respectively. They complete the work together and receive Rs. 220. How much each was paid?

Ans : The L.C.M. of 3, 6 and 9 is 18. The amount paid are in ratio
$$\frac{18}{3} : \frac{18}{6} : \frac{18}{9} = 6 : 3 : 2.$$
∴ Amount paid to Peter, Tom and John are Rs.120; Rs.60; Rs.40. respectively

7. **Some men can build a house in 15 days. If 5 more persons were to be there, it would have been built 3 days earlier. How many persons were there in the beginning?**

   Ans : $\dfrac{5 \times (15-3)}{3} = 20$ persons.

8. **A and B together can do a work in 12 days. After both worked for 8 days, A left and B completed the work in another 10 days. In how many days can A alone do the whole work?**

   Ans : After 8 days, $\dfrac{8}{12}$ work was done and balance is $\dfrac{4}{12}$ or $\dfrac{1}{3}$ work.

   That is, what work was to be done by A+B in 4 days, was done by B alone in 10 days.

   ∴ A alone can do the work in $\dfrac{3}{1} \times \dfrac{10 \times 4}{10-4} = \dfrac{120}{6} = 20$ days.

   Of course, B, alone can do the work in $10 \times \dfrac{3}{1} = 30$ days.

9. **A mason can build a tank in 10 hours. After working for 4 hours, he took a boy with him and both finished the work in another 5 hours. How long will the boy alone take to do it?**

   Ans : Man worked for a total of 9 hours. Work left was $\dfrac{1}{10}$ which was done by the boy in 5 hours.

   ∴ Boy alone can do it in $5 \times \dfrac{10}{1} = 50$ hours.

10. **Ram, who can do a work alone in 40 days, left the work after working 5 days. The balance work was completed by Gopal in 21 days. In how many days can both working together complete the work?**

    Ans : Work done by Ram was $\dfrac{5}{40}$ or $\dfrac{1}{8}$. Balance $\dfrac{7}{8}$ work was done by Gopal in 21 days.

    This balance work can be done by Ram alone in 35 days.

    ∴ Both can do the work in $\dfrac{8}{7} \times \dfrac{35 \times 21}{35+21} = \dfrac{8}{7} \times \dfrac{35 \times 21}{56}$
    $= 15$ days.

11. A can do a work in 5 days and B in 10 days separately. But, when C also joined, all the three completed the work in 2 days. How long will C take to complete the work alone?

Ans : A + B can do the work in $\dfrac{5 \times 10}{5+10} = \dfrac{50}{15} = \dfrac{10}{3}$ days.

A + B + C did it in 2 days.

So, C alone can do it in $\dfrac{\dfrac{10}{3} \times 2}{\dfrac{10}{3} - 2} = \dfrac{\dfrac{20}{3}}{\dfrac{4}{3}} = \dfrac{20}{3} \times \dfrac{3}{4} = 5$ days.

12. Babu can do a work in 8 days and Dev can do it alone in 12 days. Babu started the work and after some time Dev joined him and the work was completed in a total of 6 days. When did Dev join Babu?

Ans : Babu worked all 6 days. Work done $= \dfrac{6}{8} = \dfrac{3}{4}$ part. Balance $= \dfrac{1}{4}$ part.

Dev can do $\dfrac{1}{12}$ work in a day. So he took $\dfrac{1}{4} \times \dfrac{12}{1} = 3$ days to do the balance work.

So, he joined Babu after 6 – 3 = 3 days after.

Note : You can get Dev's time directly by $\dfrac{8-6}{8} \times 12 = 3$ days.

13. A and B can do a work separately in 30 days and 20 days respectively. After A has worked for 5 days B joined him. How many days will both take to complete the balance work?

Ans : Work done by A $= \dfrac{5}{30} = \dfrac{1}{6}$. Balance $= \dfrac{5}{6}$

Both will do the balance work in $= \dfrac{5}{6} \times \dfrac{30 \times 20}{30+20} = \dfrac{5}{6} \times \dfrac{600}{50}$

= 10 days.

14. Some workers completed $\dfrac{3}{4}$ of a work in 30 days. After 20 more persons joined them the work was completed in 6 days. How many workers were there in the beginning?

Ans : It is obvious that the full work takes 40 days, and so the balance work of $\dfrac{1}{4}$ is to be completed in 10 days by the original workers.

[80]

But, with 20 workers more the work was completed in 6 days.

∴ The workers in the beginning $= \dfrac{6 \times 20}{10-6} = \dfrac{120}{4}$

$= 30$ workers.

15. P and R can do a work separately in 30 days and 20 days respectively. P starts the work and after 5 days R joins him. Together they work for 6 days, when S joins them. All the three work for 2 days and complete the work. In how many days can S alone do the work?

   Ans : P worked for $5+6+2 = 13$ days (i.e.,) $\dfrac{13}{30}$ part.

   R worked for $6+2 = 8$ days (i.e.,) $\dfrac{8}{20}$ or $\dfrac{2}{5}$ part.

   Balance work $= 1 - \left(\dfrac{13}{30} + \dfrac{2}{5}\right) = 1 - \dfrac{25}{30} = \dfrac{5}{30}$ or $\dfrac{1}{6}$

   So, S did $\dfrac{1}{6}$ of work in 2 days.

   He can do the whole work in $\dfrac{2 \times 6}{1} = 12$ days.

16. Ravi, Gopu and Somu together can do a work in 12 days. They start the work and after 4 days Ravi left. Gopu and Somu together work and complete the work in 12 days. In how many days can Ravi alone do the entire work?

   Ans : Balance of work when Ravi left was $\dfrac{8}{12}$ or $\dfrac{2}{3}$ which was done by both Gopu and Somu in 12 days.

   ∴ Gopu and Somu can do the whole work in

   $12 \times \dfrac{3}{2} = 18$ days.

   But all the three can do the work in 12 days.

   So, Ravi alone can do it in $\dfrac{18 \times 12}{18 - 12} = \dfrac{216}{6} = 36$ days.

17. A contractor employs certain number of labourers to build a shed in a certain number of days and notices that if 3 more men were employed the whole work would have been completed in 16 days and if 2 workers were to be less, it would have taken 24 days to complete the work. How many labourers did he employ and how many days they took to complete the work?

Ans : No. of labourers = $\dfrac{16 \times 3 + 24 \times 2}{24 - 16} = \dfrac{96}{8} = 12$ Men

3 more men means $12 + 3 = 15$. If 15 persons take 16 days,

12 persons will do the work in $\dfrac{15 \times 16}{12} = 20$ days.

18. **The efficiency of John is thrice as that of Peter; and John can complete a work in 6 hours less than Peter. If both work together, in how many days can the work be completed?**

    Ans : Efficiency of J:P = 3:1, means their time Ratio is 1:3. The difference is 2. For a difference of 6 Hours the time are $\dfrac{6}{2} \times (1 : 3) = 3$ hours and 9 hours.

    ∴ Both can do the work in $\dfrac{9 \times 3}{9 + 3} = \dfrac{27}{12} = 2\dfrac{1}{4}$ hours.

19. **The efficiency of Gopal is double to that of Venu. If both together can do a work in 10 days, then in how many days Venu alone can do it?**

    Ans : That is, if Gopal takes one day, Venu will take 2 days to do the same work. So, both can do the work in $\dfrac{2 \times 1}{2 + 1} = \dfrac{2}{3}$ days.

    If both can do in 10 days, then the ratio will be $10 \times \dfrac{3}{2}$ [1:2] = 15 days (Gopal) and 30 days (Venu).

20. **A tap can fill a tank in 4 hours and another can empty it in 3 hours. When the tank is full and both taps are opened, when will the tank be emptied?**

    or

21. **A tap can fill a tank in 3 hours and another can empty it in 4 hours. When the tank is empty and both taps are opened, how long will it take to fill the tank?**

    Ans : For both $\dfrac{3 \times 4}{4 - 3} = 12$ hours.

22. **A tap can fill a tank in 20 min. and if another tap which empties the tank is also opened at the same time, the tank will be filled up in 60 min. In how many minutes can the 2nd tap empty the full tank?**

Ans : $\dfrac{60 \times 20}{60-20} = \dfrac{1200}{40} = 30$ min.

Note : Substitute the words 'empty' for 'fill' and 'fill' for 'empty', you have the question – when the 2nd tap can fill up the tank full? The method and answer are the same.

23. 2 taps can fill a tank separately in 6 min. and 8 min. and a third tap which can empty the tank is also opened along with the first two. At the same time the tank gets filled in $4\dfrac{4}{5}$ min. In how many minutes can the third tap empty the full tank?

    Ans : First two taps together can fill in $\dfrac{6 \times 8}{6+8} = \dfrac{48}{14} = \dfrac{24}{7}$ min.

    Time taken to fill when all three are opened $= \dfrac{24}{5}$ min

    ∴ Third tap can empty the full tank in $\dfrac{24}{7-5} = \dfrac{24}{2} = 12$ min.

24. From the above sum :– One tap fills the tank in 6 min., and another fills it in 8 min. A third tap empties the full tank in 12 min. If all the three taps are opened at the same time when will the tank be full?

    Ans : Filling time of 2 taps $= \dfrac{6 \times 8}{6+8} = \dfrac{48}{14} = \dfrac{24}{7}$ min.

    Emptying time $= 12$ min.

    When all three are opened tank will be full in

    $$\dfrac{2\dfrac{4}{7} \times 12}{12 - 2\dfrac{4}{7}} = \dfrac{24 \times 12}{7} \times \dfrac{7}{60} = \dfrac{24}{5} = 4\dfrac{4}{5} \text{ min.}$$

25. From the above sum:– 1st tap empties the tank in 6 min, 2nd tap empties the tank in 8 min. 3rd tap fills the tank full in 12 min. When all three are opened and the tank is full, how much time it will take for the tank to be emptied?

    Ans : Same as above – $4\dfrac{4}{5}$ min.

26. Two taps which can fill a tank in 10 min and 15 min separately, were opened at the same time. At the time when the tank was to be full, it was noticed that a third tap which empties the tank was also open and it was closed. After another $4\dfrac{1}{2}$ min., the tank was filled. How long will it take for the third tap to empty the full tank?

Ans : Both taps can fill in $\dfrac{10 \times 15}{10+15} = \dfrac{150}{25} = 6$ min.

What was emptied by the third tap in 6 min. was filled by two taps in $4\dfrac{1}{2}$ min. (i.e.,) $\dfrac{4\dfrac{1}{2}}{6}$ part was emptied in 6 min.

$= \dfrac{9}{2} \times \dfrac{1}{6} = \dfrac{3}{4}$ part in 6 min.

Full tank will be emptied in $6 \times \dfrac{4}{3} = 8$ min.

Note : Substitute the words, 'empty' for 'fill' or 'full' and 'fill or full' for 'empty', you get the question, assuming the tank was full in the beginning- How long will it take for the third tap to fill the tank?

Working is the same as above with the answer – 8 min.

✼ ✼ ✼

INTEREST

1. A sum of money doubles itself in 20 years at simple rate of interest. In how many years does it become 4 times?

    Ans : The rate of S.I. works out to 5%. When the amount becomes 4 times, it means an addition of 3 times interest.
    $$\therefore \text{Time} = \frac{300}{5} = 60 \text{ years.}$$
    From the above, it will be seen that in 40 years, the amount will become three times.

2. The S.I. on a sum of money for $2\frac{1}{2}$ years at 6% P.A. is more than the S.I. on the same money for $1\frac{1}{2}$ years at 8% P.A., by Rs.18. What is the sum?

    Ans : Difference between $6 \times 2\frac{1}{2}$ and $8 \times 1\frac{1}{2}$ is 3.
    So, the amount is $\frac{18}{3} \times 100 = $ Rs.600

3. A man borrows Rs.600 at 8% S.I. and immediately lends it to another at a higher rate of S.I. If at the end of $3\frac{1}{2}$ years he gets Rs.42 profit, at what rate he lent the amount?

    Ans : Difference of 1% on Rs.600 for $3\frac{1}{2}$ years will be Rs.21. For Rs.42, the difference in rate will be 2.
    The rate at which the amount was lent = 8 + 2 = 10%

4. A sum of Rs.3,600 is divided into 2 parts such that the interest on the Ist part at 5% S.I. for 3 years and the interest on the IInd part at 2% S.I. for 5 years are equal. What is the ratio of the two parts?

    Ans : Ist Part $5 \times 3 = 15$ IInd part $2 \times 5 = 10$
    To get the investment ratio Reverse (i.e.,) 10:15 or 2:3

    Note : The actual amount has no relevance here. If the amount is asked, it is Rs.1,440 and Rs.2,160.

5. Raman invests Rs.2,000, part at 10% S.I. and the balance at 15% S.I. If he receives an interest of Rs.460 for 2 years, how much he has invested under each head?

Ans : Interest for 1 year = Rs.230. At 10% S.I., the interest on the whole amount is Rs.200. The difference of Rs.30 in interest is got by the 5% extra on the 2nd part.

∴ 2nd Amount = $\dfrac{30}{5} \times 100$ = Rs.600

Ist part (balance) = Rs.1,400

This also gives the ratio of Investment as 14:6 (or) 7:3

6. **A sum of Rs.2,640 was invested at 8% S.I., part for 4 years, and the balance for 7 years. If the total amount received under both heads are equal, how much money was invested under each head?**

   Ans : The interest ratio on I and II part = 32 : 56

   The total amounts received are equal. So, they are in ratio (100 + 56) : (100 + 32) = 156 :132 = 13:11.

   The respective amounts are Rs.2,640 × $\dfrac{13}{24}$ = Rs.1,430 and

   II part (balance) = 1,210.

7. **A sum of Rs.5100, was invested in 3 parts, all at 10% S.I. per annum. If total amounts received after, 6,5 and 2 years respectively on the three parts are equal, how much was invested under each part?**

   Ans :

	A	B	C
Interest ratio at 10% for the 3 periods =	60 :	50 :	20

   Total amount ratio = 160:150:120 or 16:15:12

   which gives A:B = 16:15 and B:C = 15:12

   As the total amounts got are equal reverse the ratios.

   Investment - A:B = 15:16 and B:C = 12:15

   S.I.- Simple interest   C.I.- Compound Interest

   Make B common and ratio will be 45:48:60 (or) 15:16:20

   The amount invested for 6 years = $5100 \times \dfrac{15}{51}$ = Rs.1500

   5 years = Rs.1600

   2 years = Rs.2000

8. An employee invests Rs.780 at 6% S.I., and Rs.1040 at same rate of simple interest. If he gets an interest of $7\frac{1}{7}$ % on the whole sum, what was the interest rate on the second part? (Both invested for 1 year)

Ans : Amount ratio = 3:4 Equate: $\dfrac{18}{3+4}$ and $7\dfrac{1}{7}$

Interest ratio = $\dfrac{6:\Delta}{18:4\times\Delta} = \dfrac{18}{7}$ and $\dfrac{50}{7}$

Interest on 2nd part = $\dfrac{50-18}{4} = \dfrac{32}{4} = 8\%$

9. A financier lends money to three persons on S.I. Rs.250 at 3% to one, Rs.600 at 6% to the second and Rs.350 at a certain rate of interest to the third, all for one year. If he gets an interest of $6\dfrac{1}{4}$ % on the whole, what was the rate of interest paid by the third?

Ans : Amount 250:600:350 = 5 : 12 : 7 Capital ratio.
     3 : 6 : - Rate of Int.
     15 : 72 : Δ multiplied figure.

Equate as shown $\dfrac{15+72}{5+12+7}$ and $6\dfrac{1}{4} = \dfrac{87}{24}$ and $\dfrac{25}{4}$

i.e., $\dfrac{87}{24} \quad \dfrac{150}{24}$

Interest rate paid by the third man = $\dfrac{150-87}{7} = \dfrac{63}{7} = 9\%$

10. A clerk borrows Rs.650 at 5% S.I. and Rs.520 at 6% S.I. for one year. What was the rate of interest paid by him on the whole sum?

Ans : Amount ratio = 5 : 4
Rate of interest = 5 : 6 (A)
when multiplied 25 : 24 (B)

Overall Rate of interest = $\dfrac{25+24}{5+4} = \dfrac{49}{9} = 5\dfrac{4}{9}\%$

Note : To get the required rate of interest direct neither the ratio at (A) nor at (B) should be reduced.

SURA'S ❖ Solve the Problems in Short-Cut Methods

11. Gopal invests certain sum at 8% compound interest for 2 years. If he wants the same amount of interest at what rate of simple interest should he invest for the same period?

    Ans: C.I. = 8 × 2 + 3% of 8 = 16.64

    S.I. = $\dfrac{16.64}{2}$ = 8.32%

12. Basu invests Rs.1375 for one year, and Raju invests Rs.2000 for the same period at $1\dfrac{1}{2}$% higher rate of interest than Basu. If Raju got double the interest amount got by Basu, what was the rate of interest at which Basu invested his amount?

    Ans: Raju got double the amount of interest. If Basu wants the same interest, then he has to double his capital.

    So ratio of capitals = 2750 : 4000

    or = 11 : 16

    It means the interest rates are in ratio 16 : 11, a difference of 5 Units.

    So, Basu's rate = $16 \times \dfrac{1\frac{1}{2}}{3} = 16 \times \dfrac{3}{2} \times \dfrac{1}{3} = 8\%$

13. What is the interest amount on a sum of Rs.2500 at 12% Compound Interest for 2 years?

    Ans: 2 × 12 + 12% of 12 = 24 + 1.44 = 25.44%

    Interest amount = 25 × 25.44 = Rs.636

14. What sum invested grows into a total amount of Rs.8820 at 5% Compound Interest in 2 years?

    Ans: $\left[\dfrac{(100+5)^2}{100}\right] = \left(\dfrac{105}{100}\right)^2 = \left(\dfrac{21}{20}\right)^2 = \dfrac{441}{400}$

    Amount = $8820 \times \dfrac{400}{441}$ = Rs. 8000

15. A machine costing Rs.22500 depreciates in value by 20% every year. What is its value by the end of 2nd year?

    Ans: Compound reduction in value %

    = (20 + 20) − 20% of 20 = 40 − 4 = 36%

    ∴ Value of machine = Rs.22500 × $\dfrac{(100-36)}{100}$ = 225 × 64

    = Rs.14400

16. What is the amount of interest got at 5% Compound Interest on Rs.6000 for 3 years?

Ans : 5% of Rs.6000 × 3   = Rs. 900
       5% of Rs.300 × 3   = Rs. 45
       5% of Rs.15   =   0.75
                           Rs. 945.75

17. The interest amounts got for 2 years at a certain rate of simple and compound rate of interest are Rs.300 and Rs.309 respectively. What is the sum and the rate of interest?

Ans : For 2 years the respective interests are Rs.150 and Rs.159.

Rate of Interest $= \dfrac{9}{150} \times 100 = 6\%$

$\therefore$ Principal $= 150 \times \dfrac{100}{6} = Rs.2500$

18. A Banker lends a certain sum at 25% Compound Interest and gets back the amount with interest in 3 instalments of Rs.2500 each at the end of 1st, 2nd and 3rd year respectively. How much did he lend?

Ans : If Capital = 100; Capital + Interest = 125

Rs. $2500 \times \dfrac{4^3}{5^3} = Rs.1280$

Rs. $2500 \times \dfrac{4^2}{5^2} = Rs.1600$

Rs. $2500 \times \dfrac{4}{5} = Rs.2000$

Amount lent = Rs.4880

19. A sum of money was invested at 6% S.I. for 2 years. If the same amount is invested for the same period at same rate of Compound Interest it would have been Rs.7.20 more. What is the sum?

Ans : $6^2 = 36$ (i.e.) 36 paise difference on Rs.100 (Capital).

Amount $= \dfrac{720 \text{ paise}}{36 \text{ paise}} \times 100 = Rs.2000$

20. A housewife invests Rs.750 at the beginning of every year, at 4% compound interest. How much she would get at the end of 2nd year?

Ans : She has invested $2 \times 750 =$ Rs.1500
4% of Interest means Rs.30
Interest $=$ Rs.30 $+$ 30 $+$ 30 $+$ 4% of 30
$=$ Rs.91.20
Total Amount $=$ Rs.1591.20

21. A financier lends Rs.8000 for 3 years at 5% S.I. If he had charged at compound interest, on the same amount for the same period at the same rate, how much more he would have got?

Ans : Int. at 5% S.I. for 3 years on Rs.8000 $=$ Rs.1200
At C.I. rate he would have got more
5% of 1200 $=$ Rs.60
Int. rate 5
Time $\dfrac{5}{3}$ % of 60
$= \dfrac{5}{300} \times 60 =$ Re. 1   Rs.61 more.

22. A worker borrows a certain amount at 10% C.I. per annum and clears the loan in 2 equal annual instalments of Rs.484 each. How much did he borrow?

Ans : If P $=$ 100, A $=$ Rs.110
Go back from 2nd year to 1st year.
$484 \times \dfrac{100}{110} =$ Rs.440
$440 \times \dfrac{100}{110} =$ Rs.400
Borrowed Amount $=$ Rs.840

23. Ram borrows Rs.2120 at 12% Compound Interest and clears the loan in 2 equal annual instalments. What was the amount of each instalment?

Ans : Each year he clears part of capital and part of interest.
12% interest means for Rs.100 capital, total amount
$=$ Rs.112
Ratio $=$ 100 : 112 $=$ 25 : 28 (Total 53 units)
1st year cleared $=$ Rs.2120 $\times \dfrac{25}{53}$ $+$ Int. on Rs.2120 at 12%
$=$ Rs.1000 $+$ Rs.254.40 $=$ Rs.1254.40
which is the instalment amount.

The above also gives total amount paid = Rs.2508.80 and the interest amount = 388.80

24. A teacher buys a colour T.V. for Rs.11256 at $8\frac{1}{3}$% Compound Interest and repays the amount in 3 equal annual instalments, at the end of every year. What is the amount of instalment?

    Ans : $8\frac{1}{3}$% means $\frac{1}{12}$. If Capital is Rs.12 total amount = Rs.13
    Instalment amount =
    $$\frac{11256 \times 13^3}{12(12^2 + 13^2 + 12 \times 13)} = \frac{11256 \times 169 \times 13}{12(144 + 169 + 156)}$$
    $$= \frac{11256 \times 169 \times 13}{12 \times 469} = 338 \times 13 = Rs.4394$$

25. Raman invests a sum of Rs.900 at 8% S.I. and Gopi invests a sum of Rs.1200 at $3\frac{1}{2}$% S.I. After how much time will they both have equal amounts in their accounts?

    Ans : Difference of Interest in one year
    $= (9 \times 8) - (12 \times 3\frac{1}{2}) = 72 - 42 = Rs.30$
    To cover a difference of (1200 − 900) = Rs.300
    Time of investment $= \frac{300}{30} = 10$ years.

26. A sum of Rs.8000 was invested, part at 10% compound interest and the balance at 8% S.I. If at the end of 2nd year, the total amount got was Rs.9505, how much was invested under each head?

    Ans : For 2 years the C.I. rate = 2 × 10 + 10% of 10 = 21%
    For 2 years the S.I. rate = 2 × 8 = 16%
    Difference = 5%
    Total Interest = Rs.1505
    If invested whole amount at S.I, interest
    $= 8000 \times \frac{16}{100} = Rs.1280$
    ∴ The difference of (Rs.1505 − Rs.1280) = Rs.225 is due to the 5% difference shown above.

∴ Amount invested under C.I = $\frac{225}{5} \times 100$ = Rs.4500.

Balance invested at S.I. = Rs.3500

27. A sum invested at 5% S.I. grows to Rs.504 in 4 years. How much the same amount will grow into at 10% S.I. in $2\frac{1}{2}$ years?

Ans : Ratio of totals $100 + (5 \times 4) : 100 + 10 \times (2\frac{1}{2})$

= 120 : 125 = 24 : 25

∴ The amount = $504 \times \frac{25}{24} = 25 \times 21$ = Rs.525

28. A man invests some amount and receives $\frac{25}{36}$ of his capital as interest (S.I.) after some years. 1If the time invested for is equal to the rate of interest, what is the rate of interest?

Ans : Very simple. $\frac{\sqrt{25 \times 100}}{36} = \frac{50}{6} = 8\frac{1}{3}$% (for $8\frac{1}{3}$ years)

Note: The capital actually invested makes no difference.

Simpler is: $\frac{\sqrt{25}}{36} = \frac{5}{6}$ Multiply 5 by 10 and divide by 6

= $\frac{50}{6} = 8\frac{1}{3}$%.

❀ ❀ ❀

SIMPLIFICATION

VBODMAS Rules

V - Vinculum means bar $\overline{(5-3)}$
B - Brackets
First calculation ( )
Second calculation { }
Third calculation [ ]
O - of
D - Division
M - Multiplication
A - Addition
S - Subtraction

Squares 1 to 30

$1^2 = 1$	$11^2 = 121$	$21^2 = 441$
$2^2 = 4$	$12^2 = 144$	$22^2 = 484$
$3^2 = 9$	$13^2 = 169$	$23^2 = 529$
$4^2 = 16$	$14^2 = 196$	$24^2 = 576$
$5^2 = 25$	$15^2 = 225$	$25^2 = 625$
$6^2 = 36$	$16^2 = 256$	$26^2 = 676$
$7^2 = 49$	$17^2 = 289$	$27^2 = 729$
$8^2 = 64$	$18^2 = 324$	$28^2 = 784$
$9^2 = 81$	$19^2 = 361$	$29^2 = 841$
$10^2 = 100$	$20^2 = 400$	$30^2 = 900$

Cubes 1 to 30

$1^3 = 1$	$11^3 = 1331$	$21^3 = 9261$
$2^3 = 8$	$12^3 = 1728$	$22^3 = 10648$
$3^3 = 27$	$13^3 = 2197$	$23^3 = 12167$
$4^3 = 64$	$14^3 = 2744$	$24^3 = 13824$
$5^3 = 125$	$15^3 = 3375$	$25^3 = 15625$
$6^3 = 216$	$16^3 = 4096$	$26^3 = 17576$
$7^3 = 343$	$17^3 = 4913$	$27^3 = 19683$
$8^3 = 512$	$18^3 = 5832$	$28^3 = 21952$
$9^3 = 729$	$19^3 = 6859$	$29^3 = 24389$
$10^3 = 1000$	$20^3 = 8000$	$30^3 = 27000$

❈ Solve the Problems in Short-Cut Methods

Table 1:

D/N	1	2	3	4	5	6	7	8	9	10
1	100	200	300	400	500	600	700	800	900	1000
2	50	100	150	200	250	300	350	400	450	500
3	33.33	66.66	100							
4	25	50	75	100						
5	20	40	60	80	100					
6	16.66	33.33	50	66.66	83.33	100				
7	14.28	28.56	42.85	57.14	71.42	85.71	100			
8	12.5	25	37.5	50	62.5	75	87.5	100		
9	11.11	22.22	33.33	44.44	55.55	66.66	77.7	88.8	100	
10	10	20	30	40	50	60	70	80	90	100
11	9.09	18.18	27.27	36.36	45.45	54.54	63.6	72.7	81.8	90.9
12	8.33	16.66	25	33.33	41.66	50	58.3	66.6	75	83.3
13	7.69	15.38	23.07	30.76	38.45	46.14	53.83	61.52	69.21	76.9
14	7.14	14.28	21.42	28.57	35.71	42.85	49.98	57.12	64.26	71.4
15	6.66	13.33	20	26.66	33.33	40	46.6	53.3	60	66.6
16	6.25	12.5	18.75	25	31.25	37.5	43.7	50	56.2	62.5

D stands for Denominator
N stands for Numerator

Table 2:

Numbers	If a Number
Divisible by 2	End with 0,2,4,6,8 are divisible by 2
Divisible by 3	Sum of its digits is divisible by 3
Divisible by 4	Last two digit divisible by 4
Divisible by 5	Ends with 0 or 5
Divisible by 6	Divides by Both 2 & 3
Divisible by 8	Last 3 digit divide by 8
Divisible by 10	End with 0
Divisible by 11	[Sum of its digit in odd places-Sum of its digits in even places] = 0 or multiple of 11

SURA'S ❈ Solve the Problems in Short-Cut Methods

1. 18.18% of 1331 + 41.66% of 600 = ?

    Ans : In this type of simplification problems we shall convert percentage values into fraction. (Refer Table)

    $\frac{2}{11} \times 1331 + \frac{5}{12} \times 600$

    = 242 + 250

    = 492

2. 16.66% of 144 + 27.27% of 1331 – 6.25% of 32 = ?

    Ans : = $\frac{2}{12} \times 144 + \frac{3}{11} \times 1331 - \frac{1}{16} \times 32$

    = 24 + 363 – 2

    = 385

3. $\sqrt{484} + \sqrt[3]{1728} - \sqrt{196} + \sqrt{2744}$ = ?

    Ans : In this type of problems, directly substitute the square root & cube root values. (Memorize 1 to 30 square root & cube root values)

    = 22 + 12 – 14 + 14

    = 34

4. $\sqrt{841} + \sqrt{729} + \sqrt{24389} - \sqrt{10648}$

    Ans : = 29 + 27 + 29 – 22

    = 63

5. 60% of 130 + 20% of 120 + 125% of 64 = ?

    A) 190
    B) 193
    C) 182
    D) 176

    Ans : To solve this type of problems within 30 second we have to add the all digits of the percentage, base and reduce it to a single digit. Example:

    We can write, 60% of 130 + 20% of 120 + 125% of 64 as

    6 × 4 + 2 × 3 + 8 × 1 (Omit zero)

    = 6 + 6 + 8

    = 2

    But, answer for this problem is not '2'. We have to find the answer from the given options.

By adding the options,

A) 190 = 1 ✗

B) 193 = 4 ✗

C) 182 = 2 ✓

D) 176 = 5 ✗

Here, in the option C, 2 is matching, so the answer is 182.

6. **45% of 360 + 120% of 90 = ?**

   A) 240   **B)** 250   **C)** 270   **D)** 230

   Ans : $9 \times 9 + 3 \times 9 = 9$

   $9 + 9 = 9$

   From options:

   A) 240 = 6 ✗

   B) 250 = 7 ✗

   C) 270 = 9 ✓

   D) 230 = 5 ✗

7. **37.5% of 80% of 730 + 160% of 250 – ? = 120% of 400**

   A) 129   **B)** 139   **C)** 149   **D)** 159

   Ans : $\Rightarrow 6 \times 8 \times 1 + 7 \times 7 - 3 \times 4$

   $= 3 + 4 - 3$

   $= 4$

   From options:

   A) 129 = 3 ✗

   B) 139 = 4 ✓

   C) 149 = 5 ✗

   D) 159 = 6 ✗

   Ans = 139

8. **25% of $\sqrt[3]{4096}$ + 75% of $\sqrt[3]{21952}$ = ?**

   Ans : $= \dfrac{1}{4} \times 16 + \dfrac{3}{4} \times 28$

   $= 4 + 21$

   $= 25$

9. $8^7 \times 2^6 \div 8^{2.4} \times 8^{1.4} = 8^?$

   Ans : In this type of sums, we have to convert base uniformly.

   $8^7 \times 2^6 \div 8^{2.4} \times 8^{1.4} = 8^x$

   $8^7 \times 8^2 \div 8^{2.4} \times 8^{1.4} = 8^x$

   $8^{7 + 2 - 2.4 + 1.4} = 8^x$

   $8^8 = 8^x$

   $x = 8$

10. $(8 \times 8)^5 \div (512 \div 8)^2 \times (8 \times 64)^3 = (8)^{?+5}$

    Ans : $(8 \times 8)^5 \div \left(\dfrac{512}{8}\right)^2 \times (8^3)^3 = (8)^{x+5}$

    $8^{10} \div 8^4 \times 8^9 = (8)^{x+5}$

    $8^{15} = (8)^{x+5}$

    $x = 10$

11. 49.98% of $599.9 = x^2 + \sqrt{841.01} + 46$

    A) 16   B) 14   C) 17   D) 15

    Ans : Here, we don't have to take the values as such. We can round it off to avoid decimal. Follow the steps to understand.

    $\Rightarrow$ 50% of $600 = x^2 + \sqrt{841} + 46$

    $\Rightarrow 300 - 29 - 46 = x^2$

    $\Rightarrow 255 = x^2$

    $\Rightarrow x = 15$

12. $3.99^3 + (7.01 \times 1.98) + x = 213.02$

    A) 140   B) 135   C) 120   D) 121

    Ans : $\Rightarrow 43 + 14 + x = 213$

    $\Rightarrow x = 213 - 79$

    $\Rightarrow x = 134 \simeq 135$

13. Find the value: $\dfrac{\sqrt{5} + \sqrt{3}}{\sqrt{5} - \sqrt{3}}$

    Ans : In the given question, if the numerator & denominator is same (sign may be different), here we can apply shortcut method & find the answer easily.

Step 1:

$$\frac{x+y}{x-y} = \frac{5+3}{5-3}$$

[**Note:** Here, $x = 5, y = 3$]

Step 2:

Frame the equation like given below:

$$\boxed{\frac{x+y}{x-y} + \frac{2\sqrt{xy}}{x-y}}$$

$$\Rightarrow \frac{8}{2} + \frac{2\sqrt{15}}{2}$$

Ans $= 4 + \sqrt{15}$

14. Find the value of $\dfrac{(23+56)^2 - (23-56)^2}{23 \times 53}$.

Ans : In this type of question, take any two numbers instead of 23 & 56. We shall take 2 & 3.

$$\frac{(2+3)^2 - (2-3)^2}{2 \times 3}$$

$$\Rightarrow \frac{25-1}{6} \Rightarrow \frac{24}{6}$$

Ans $= 4$

∴ You can cross check by using the original values in the question.

15. Simplify $\dfrac{(893+786)^2 - (893-786)^2}{(893 \times 786)}$

Ans : We shall take 2 & 5 instead of 893 & 786. (You can take any small value)

$$\Rightarrow \frac{(2+5)^2 - (2-5)^2}{(2 \times 5)}$$

$$\Rightarrow \frac{49-9}{10}$$

$$\Rightarrow \frac{40}{10} = \textbf{Ans} = 4$$

HCF AND LCM OF NUMBERS

Important Formulas:
- LCM × HCF = Product of the two numbers
- LCM = $\dfrac{\text{Product of two numbers}}{\text{HCF}}$
- HCF = $\dfrac{\text{Product of two numbers}}{\text{LCM}}$
- First number = $\dfrac{\text{LCM} \times \text{HCF}}{\text{Second number}}$
- Second number = $\dfrac{\text{LCM} \times \text{HCF}}{\text{First number}}$
- LCM of fraction = $\dfrac{\text{LCM of numerators}}{\text{HCF of denominators}}$
- HCF of fraction = $\dfrac{\text{HCF of numerators}}{\text{LCM of denominators}}$

Important Points:
- For two or more prime numbers, the HCF is 1.
- For two or more prime numbers, the LCM is equal to their products.

1. **Three numbers are in the ratio of 3 : 4 : 5 and their LCM is 2400. Their HCF is ....**

   Ans : In traditional method we have to frame equation as $3x : 4x : 5x$ and find LCM. After finding the value of x, we have to substitute in that equation.

   Now, note the short cut method:
   Multiply the given ratio $3 \times 4 \times 5 = 60$. Divide the LCM by 60.

   (i.e.) $\dfrac{2400}{60} = 40$

   ∴ HCF of the numbers = 40

2. **If the ratio of two numbers is 3 : 4 and their HCF is 4 then their LCM is ....**

   Ans : Multiply the given ratio 3 : 4
   $\Rightarrow 3 \times 4 = 12$

   Note: [If HCF is asked use division. If LCM is asked use multiplication]

Here, multiply 12 with 4 (HCF)
Answer = 48

3. **If the ratio of two numbers is 5 : 6, and their LCM is 480, then their HCF is ....**

   Ans : Multiply the given ratio 5 : 6
   $\Rightarrow 30$
   Here, HCF is asked, so divide the LCM by 30.
   $$\frac{480}{30} = 16$$
   Answer = 16

4. **If the ratio of two numbers is 2 : 3 and their LCM is 48. Find sum of the numbers.**

   Ans : Observe the question carefully, here, in the question sum of the numbers is asked.
   Given LCM is 48.
   Simply, divide the LCM by the ratios individually
   (i.e) $\frac{48}{2}$ & $\frac{48}{3}$
   = 24 & 16
   Here, sum of the numbers is asked. Hence, 24 + 16 = 40
   Answer = 40

5. **Find the LCM of 2 × 3 × 5 × 7, 3 × 5 × 7 × 11.**

   Ans : In this type of sums, lengthy calculations are involved. It needs more time. To crack these types of questions within 15 seconds you must familiar with the shortcuts. Forget the lengthy calculations. Just write down the numbers in the below format.

   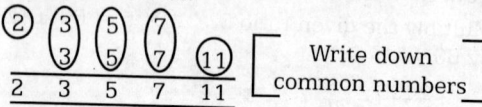

   [Write down common numbers]

   ∴ The answer is 2 3 5 7 11.

6. **If product of given three numbers is 1875 and their HCF is 5, then their LCM is**

   Ans : $\dfrac{1875}{5 \times 5}$ [To find LCM, write down the product of the given number and divide it by the HCF two times]

   Answer = 75

7. Find the HCF of $25ab^3c$, $100a^2bc$, $125ab$

   Ans : **Step : 1**

a	b^3	c
a^2	b	c
a	b	
a	b	

   $\begin{bmatrix} \textbf{Step : 1} \\ \text{Take out the common letters from the} \\ \text{three rows. That letter must present in} \\ \text{all the three rows} \end{bmatrix}$

   Step : 2

   a^1, b^1 $\begin{bmatrix} \textbf{Step : 2} \\ \text{In case of power, select the lowest value} \end{bmatrix}$

   We know that HCF of 25, 100, 125 is 25.

   ∴ Ans = 25 ab

8. A worker was engaged for a certain number of days, but he remained absent for some days and was paid Rs. 1,387. Had he worked all the days, he would have earned Rs. 1752. How many days did he work for?

   Ans : HCF of 1387 = 73 × 19
   HCF of 1752 = 73 × 24

   ∴ Earnings per day = Rs. 73

   $\Rightarrow \dfrac{1387}{73}$

   = 19 days

9. Find the LCM of a^3b^4, ab^3 and a^2b^7.

   Ans : **Step : 1**

a^3	b^4
a	b^5
a^2	b^7
a	b	[Common letter]

   Step : 2

   Ans: $a^3 b^7$ (For LCM, take the largest power)

10. If HCF of p & q is x and q = xy, find the LCM of p and q from the following:

    Ans : p × q = x

    $\Rightarrow$ p × xy = x

    = py

MENSURATION

2-DIMENSIONAL FIGURES AND FORMULAS

Rectangle
- Area of a Rectangle = Length × Breadth
- Perimeter of a Rectangle = 2 × (Length × Breadth)
- Length of the Diagonal = $\sqrt{\text{Length}^2 + \text{Breadth}^2}$

Square
- Area of a square = (side)^2
- Perimeter of a square = 4 × side
- Length of a the Diagonal = $\sqrt{2}$ × side
- If diagonal value is given, Area of square = $\dfrac{d^2}{2}$

Parallelogram

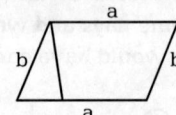

- Area of parallelogram = a × h
- Perimeter of parallelogram = 2(a + b)

Trapezium

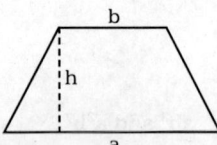

- Area of Trapezium = $\dfrac{1}{2}h(a+b)$
- Perimeter of Trapezium = Sum of its four sides

Rhombus

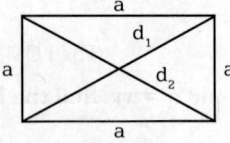

- Area of a Rhombus = $\dfrac{1}{2} \times d_1 \times d_2$
- Perimeter of a Rhombus = Sum of its four sides

Triangle

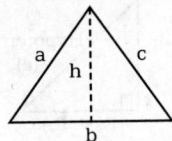

- Area of Triangle = $\frac{1}{2}(b \times h)$
- Perimeter of Triangle = a + b + c

Scalene Triangle

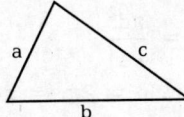

- Area of Triangle = $\sqrt{S(S-a)(S-b)(S-c)}$

  Where $S = \frac{a+b+c}{2}$

- Perimeter of Triangle = a + b + c

  Scalene Triangle has No equal sides and No equal angles

Equilateral Triangle

Area of Equilateral Triangle = $\left(\frac{\sqrt{3}}{4}\right) \times \text{side}^2$

Perimeter of Equilateral Triangle = 3 × side

Equilateral Triangle has Three equal sides and three equal angles.

Isosceles Triangle

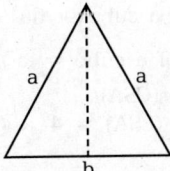

- Area of Isosceles Triangle = $\frac{1}{2} \times b \times h$
- Perimeter of Isosceles Triangle = 2a + b
- Isosceles Triangle has Two equal sides and two equal angles.

Right angled Triangle

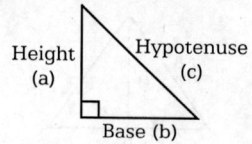

- Area of Right angled Triangle = $\frac{1}{2} \times$ base $\times$ height
- Perimeter of Right angled Triangle = a + b + c

Formulas for Circle and Semicircle

- Area of circle = $\pi r^2 = \dfrac{\pi d^2}{4}$
- Circumference of a circle = $2\pi r = \pi d$
- Area of semi circle = $\dfrac{(\pi r^2)}{2}$
- Circumference of semicircle = πr
- Perimeter of the semicircle = $(\pi r + d)$
- Length of an arc = $\dfrac{2\pi r \theta}{360°}$

  θ = central angle in degree

- Area of a sector = $\dfrac{1}{2} \times$ length of arc $\times r \left(\dfrac{\pi r^2 \theta}{360°}\right)$

3-DIMENSIONAL FIGURES AND FORMULAS

Cube

- Volume of a cube = (side)^3 = a^3
- Total surface area of a cube = $6a^2$
- Length of Diagonal of a cube = $a\sqrt{3}$
- Curved Surface Area (CSA)/ Lateral Surface Area (LSA) = $4 \times$ (side)^2

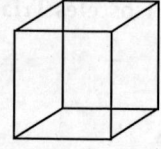

Cuboid

- Total surface area of cuboid = $2(lb + bh + hl)$
- Curved Surface Area (CSA)/ Lateral Surface Area (LSA) = 2 height (Length + Breadth)

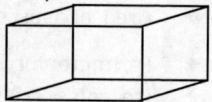

- Volume of cube = $l \times b \times h$
- Length of Diagonal = $\sqrt{l^2 + b^2 + h^2}$

Cone

- Slant height of cone = $l = \sqrt{h^2 + r^2}$
- Curved surface area of a cone = $\pi r l$
- Total surface area of a cone = $\pi r(r + l)$
- Volume of right circular cone = $\dfrac{1}{3}\pi r^2 h$

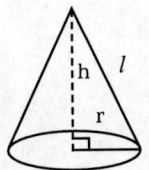

Cylinder

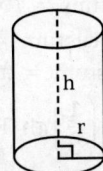

- Curved surface area of a cylinder = $2\pi rh$
- Total surface area of a cylinder = $2\pi r(r + h)$
- Volume of a cylinder = $\pi r^2 h$

Sphere

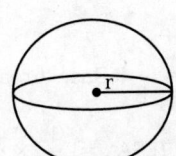

- Volume of sphere = $\dfrac{4}{3}\pi r^3 = \left(\dfrac{1}{6}\right)\pi d^3$
- Surface area of sphere = $4\pi r^2 = \pi d^2$
- If a sphere is cut into 'n' parts, then total surface area of 'n' parts = $4\pi r^2 + n\pi r^2$
- For a spherical shell if R and r are outer and inner radii respectively, then volume of a shell = $\dfrac{4}{3}\pi(R^3 - r^3)$

Hemisphere

- Volume of hemisphere = $\dfrac{2}{3}\pi r^3$
- Curved surface area = $2\pi r^2$
- Total surface area = $3\pi r^2$

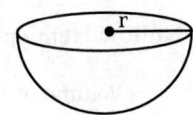

Hollow Cylinder

Volume of hollow cylinder = $\pi h(R^2 - r^2)$

(R = Radius of cylinder, r = radius of cavity)

Frustum of a Right circular cone

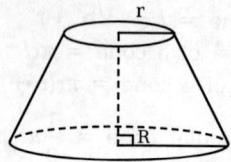

- Slant height of the frustum = $l = \sqrt{h^2 + (R-r)^2}$
- Curved surface area of frustum = $\pi(R + r)l$
- Total surface area of frustum = $\pi(R + r)l + \pi(R^2 + r^2)$
- Volume of a frustum = $\left(\dfrac{1}{3}\right)\pi h\left(R^2 + r^2 + Rr\right)$
- **Curved surface area** - This is the total area of all curved surfaces.
- **Lateral surface area** - This is the whole area of the surface excluding the top and bottom.
- **Total surface area** - This is the total area of the object's surfaces, including the bases.

Pyramid

- Volume of pyramid = $\dfrac{1}{3} \times$ Base Area $\times$ height
- Lateral Surface Area (LSA) = $\dfrac{1}{2} \times$ Perimeter of base $\times$ Slant height
- Total surface area = LSA + Area of Base

Prism

- Volume of Prism = Base Area $\times$ Height
- Lateral surface area = Perimeter of Base $\times$ Height
- Total surface area = LSA + 2 $\times$ Area of Base

Hollow sphere

Volume of hollow sphere = $\dfrac{4}{3}\pi\left(R^3 - r^3\right)$

Hollow Hemisphere

Volume of Hollow Hemisphere = $\dfrac{2}{3}\pi R^3 \times \dfrac{2}{3}\pi r^3$

1. **The ratio of the volumes of two spheres is 8 : 27. Find the ratio of their radius.**

    Ans : In usual method, we must memorize lot of area and volume formulas. But, here we are going to apply a trick that needs no formula & lengthy calculations.

    Simply memorize the below steps:

    Single dimension $\Rightarrow$ Radius/Side $\Rightarrow$ a : b
    2 dimension $\Rightarrow$ Area $\Rightarrow$ $a^2 : b^2$
    3 dimension $\Rightarrow$ Volume $\Rightarrow$ $a^3 : b^3$

    We know, volume is a three dimensional figure. If it is three dimensional, simply take cube root of the given value.

    Here, $\sqrt{8} : \sqrt{27}$

    Ans = 2 : 3

    [You can cross check the answer by using sphere formula]

2. **The ratio of the volumes of two cubes is 27 : 64. Find the ratio of their surface area.**

    Ans : Volume $\Rightarrow$ 3 dimension = 27 : 64
    Side $\Rightarrow$ 1 dimension (Take cube root) = 3 : 4

    In the question surface area is asked which is two dimension, simply square the sides (i.e) 3 : 4 $\Rightarrow$ 9 : 16

    ∴ Ans = 9 : 16

3. **The ratio of the surface area of two cylinders is 16 : 49. Find the ratio of their volume.**

    Ans : Surface area : 2 dimension = 16 : 49
    Radius : 1 dimension (Take square root) = 4 : 7
    Volume : 3 dimension = 64 : 343

    ∴ Ans = 64 : 343

4. **The surface area of 2 spheres are in the ratio 4 : 9. Then the ratio of their volume will be?**

    Ans : Surface area : 2 dimension = 4 : 9
    Radius : 1 dimension = 2 : 3
    Volume : 3 dimension = 8 : 27

    Ans = 8 : 27

5. **What would be the measure of the diagonal of a square whose area is equal to 882 cm²?**

    Ans : We know that diagonal = $\sqrt{2}a$
    $a^2 = 882$ (given)
    $= \sqrt{2} \times \sqrt{2 \times 441}$
    $\Rightarrow 2 \times 21$
    Diagonal = 42 cm

6. **Find the area of the iron sheet required to prepare a cone 24 cm high with base radius 7 cm.**

    A) 704 cm²   B) 702 cm²   C) 700 cm²   D) 668 cm²

    Ans : In this type of sums, we shall follow "π" short cut method. (i.e) If the formula π involved in the question. We can find the answer from the options itself.

    Here, volume of cone = $\dfrac{1}{3} \pi r^2 h$

    If "π" formula is involved, divide all the given options by "11". If any one of the options perfectly divisible by "11" then that is your answer.

    In this question option A = 704, is divisible by "11". So the answer is 704 cm².

    [**Note:** You can cross check it by usual method]

7. **A hollow cylindrical iron pipe has length 35 cm. Its outer and inner diameters are 10 cm and 8 cm respectively. Find the weight of the pipe if 1 cu.m of iron weighs 7 gm.**

    A) 6.93 kg   B) 7.75 kg   C) 7.83 kg   D) 7.93 kg

    Ans : We know that volume of cylindrical pipe = $\pi h (R^2 - r^2)$
    So we can apply "π" short cut.
    In the given option 6.93 (omit decimal i.e. take it as 693) is divisible by 11.
    Ans = 6.93 kg

8. **Surface area of hemisphere is 2772 cm² then the total surface area of hemisphere?**

    A) 4158 cm²   B) 3172 cm²   C) 3882 cm²   D) 4258 cm²

    Ans : By applying "π" short cut, option A = 4158 cm² is divisible by 11.
    So the answer will be 4158 cm²

≈ ≈ ≈ ≈ ≈